CW01337961

Iceland Travel Guide

Captivating Adventures through Must-See Places, Local Culture, Icelandic Landmarks, Hidden Gems, and More

© Copyright 2024 - All rights reserved.

The content contained within this book may not be reproduced, duplicated, or transmitted without direct written permission from the author or the publisher.

Under no circumstances will any blame or legal responsibility be held against the publisher, or author, for any damages, reparation, or monetary loss due to the information contained within this book, either directly or indirectly.

Legal Notice:

This book is copyright protected. It is only for personal use. You cannot amend, distribute, sell, use, quote, or paraphrase any part, or the content within this book, without the consent of the author or publisher.

Disclaimer Notice:

Please note the information contained within this document is for educational and entertainment purposes only. All effort has been executed to present accurate, up-to-date, reliable, and complete information. No warranties of any kind are declared or implied. Readers acknowledge that the author is not engaging in the rendering of legal, financial, medical, or professional advice. The content within this book has been derived from various sources. Please consult a licensed professional before attempting any techniques outlined in this book.

By reading this document, the reader agrees that under no circumstances is the author responsible for any losses, direct or indirect, that are incurred as a result of the use of the information contained within this document, including, but not limited to, errors, omissions, or inaccuracies.

Table of Contents

INTRODUCTION 1
CHAPTER 1: GET TO KNOW ICELAND 4
CHAPTER 2: TO AND FROM THE AIRPORT 21
CHAPTER 3: REYKJAVÍK: THE CAPITAL 30
CHAPTER 4: REYKJANES PENINSULA, THE GOLDEN CIRCLE AND THE SOUTH COAST 50
CHAPTER 5: WESTERN ICELAND 83
CHAPTER 6: THE WESTFJORDS 105
CHAPTER 7: NORTH ICELAND 121
CHAPTER 8: EAST ICELAND 141
CHAPTER 9: ITINERARIES AND PROGRAMS 150
BONUS CHAPTER: USEFUL ICELANDIC SURVIVAL PHRASES 159
APPENDIX: UNVEILING TREASURES FROM A TO Z 163
CHECK OUT ANOTHER BOOK IN THE SERIES 172
REFERENCES 173

Introduction

Iceland, sculpted by ancient giants, where waterfalls thunder into turquoise fjords and glaciers whisper secrets of the ice age. This country is a tapestry woven with volcanic fire and glacial tears. Here, the horizon dances with the aurora borealis, and the air vibrates with raw, untamed beauty. But Iceland feels like a riddle wrapped in an enigma. How do you navigate its vast, untamed landscapes? Where do you find the hidden gems that escape the tourist trail? And how do you capture the essence of this Nordic wonderland without feeling lost in the wilderness?

The map below shows the areas covered in this book. The numbers indicate the chapter numbers.

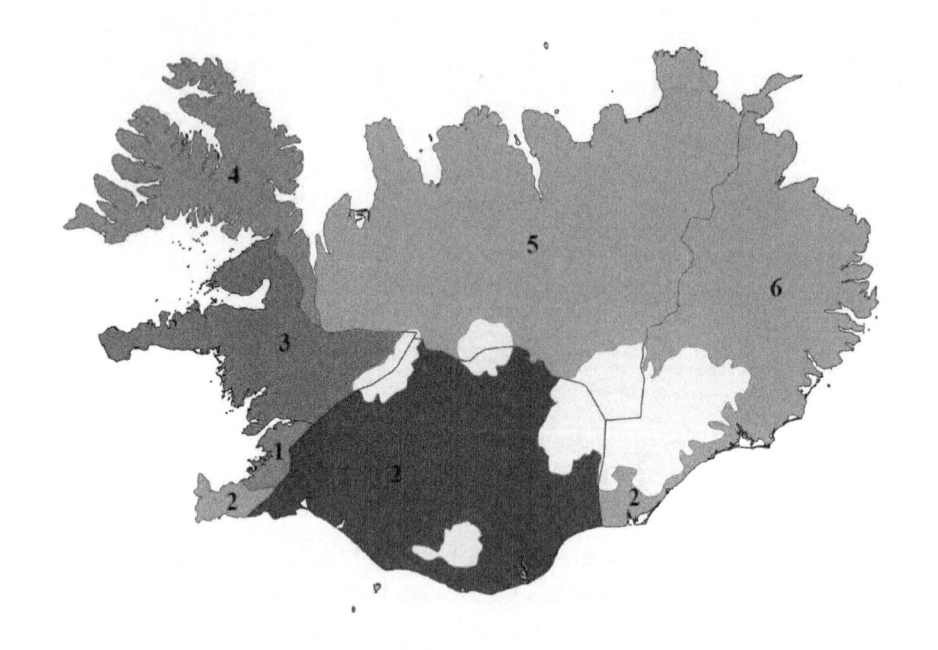

The Regions of Iceland.

1 – Reykjavik

2- Reykjanes Peninsula, the Golden Cirle and the South Coast

3- Western Iceland

4- The Westfjords

5- North Iceland

6- East Iceland

This is where the Iceland Travel Guide steps in, your trusty companion on this unforgettable adventure. Forget the jargon-filled guidebooks and cookie-cutter itineraries. This book is your passport to a simple, accessible Iceland, crafted for the curious beginner seeking an experience beyond the postcards. Within these pages, you'll find:

- **Actionable Ideas and Hands-On Methods**: No more dry words. This guide will show you how to navigate Iceland's ever-changing weather, pack like a pro, and conquer glaciers like a seasoned explorer.
- **Budget-Savvy Insights:** From cozy guesthouses to affordable dining, it will help you draw up an Icelandic adventure that's kind to your wallet without sacrificing an ounce of magic.

- **Local Secrets Revealed:** Forget the tourist traps. This book will unveil hidden waterfalls, charming villages, and geothermal havens known only to those who genuinely understand Iceland's soul.
- **A Storyteller's Guide to Photography:** Capture the emerald fire of the Northern Lights, Gullfoss's thunderous roar, and the otherworldly beauty of Jökulsárlón glacier lagoon with some unique photography tips and insider locations.

This guide isn't just a book of practicalities. It's an invitation to awaken your inner explorer. In no time, you'll be hiking through volcanic landscapes, kayaking through glacial lagoons, and soaking in milky-blue geothermal pools. Prepare for the earth's fiery heart to warm you from within.

This Guide Is Your Chance To:
- Unravel the mysteries of Reykjavik, Iceland's vibrant capital, where Viking history meets contemporary cool.
- Journey along the Reykjanes Peninsula and the South Coast, marveling at the power of waterfalls like Seljalandsfoss and Skógafoss before stepping onto the black sand beaches of Reynisdrangar.
- Explore the otherworldly beauty of West Iceland, home to Snæfellsjökull glacier, the crown jewel of the Snaefellsnes Peninsula.
- Venture into the rugged Westfjords, a land of dramatic cliffs, hidden fjords, and puffin colonies teeming with life.
- Discover the hidden gems of North Iceland, from the geothermal haven of Mývatn to the lunar-like landscapes of Askja caldera.
- Unwind in the serene East Iceland, where glaciers meet the sea and quaint fishing villages whisper tales of the past.

Each chapter is your key to unlocking a new facet of Iceland's magic. So, pack your bags, unleash your inner adventurer, and let the Iceland Travel Guide be your compass as you embark on a journey that will leave you breathless, inspired, and forever changed.

Turn the page and let Iceland's magic begin!

Chapter 1: Get to Know Iceland

Iceland wears many crowns, each glittering with an allure that attracts travelers from all over the world. Before you embark on your Nordic adventure, get to know Iceland and what it has to offer. Nestled in the North Atlantic, just south of the Arctic Circle, Iceland is a paradox in paradise. You'll find volcanoes erupting fiery lava into glaciers carved by ancient ice. It's not uncommon to spot moss-carpeted lava fields cradling turquoise lagoons warmed by the earth's molten heart. This is the essence of Iceland, a land where fire and ice tango in a breathtaking dance of nature's extremes.

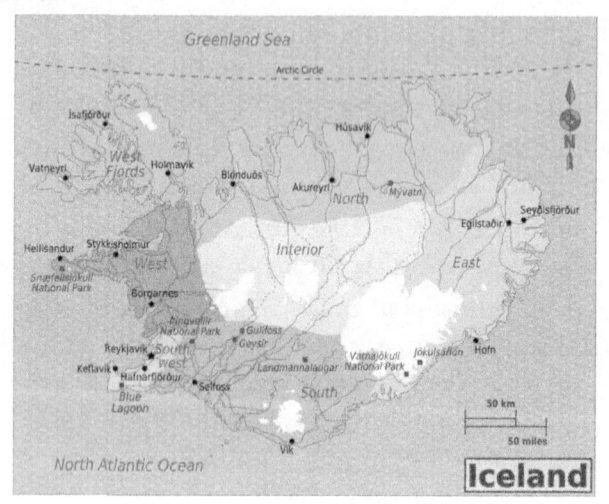

Iceland map.
Burmesedays, CC BY-SA 3.0 <https://creativecommons.org/licenses/by-sa/3.0>, via Wikimedia Commons. https://commons.wikimedia.org/wiki/File:Iceland_Regions_map_2.png

A Map of Majesty: Unveiling Iceland's Breathtaking Landscapes

Iceland is a land where fire dances with ice, and nature paints landscapes in tones of emerald, sapphire, and fiery red. It's a place where glaciers whisper ancient secrets, volcanoes erupt with molten fury, and waterfalls thunder into turquoise fjords. However, to truly grasp its majesty, you need a map – one that traces the contours of its stunning geography, region by region.

A Tapestry of Eight Lands

As you unfurl the map, it reveals eight distinct threads woven into a tapestry of hidden wonders:

- **Southwest Iceland:** Reykjavik, the vibrant capital, pulsates with energy, while the Golden Circle dazzles with geothermal marvels like the Gullfoss waterfall and Strokkur geyser. Black sand beaches and the ethereal Jökulsárlón glacier lagoon, where icebergs shimmer like diamonds, add to the drama.

The Gullfoss waterfall.
Pierre-Selim Huard, CC BY 4.0 <https://creativecommons.org/licenses/by/4.0>, via Wikimedia Commons. https://commons.wikimedia.org/wiki/File:Iceland_-_2017-02-22_-_Gullfoss_-_3684.jpg

- **South Coast:** Witness thunderous waterfalls like Skógafoss and Seljalandsfoss, stand in awe of the volcanic cliffs of Reynisdrangar, and explore the charming village of Vík í Mýrdal, nestled amidst Reynisdrangar sea stacks.

Reynisdrangar.
Spike, CC BY-SA 4.0 <https://creativecommons.org/licenses/by-sa/4.0>, via Wikimedia Commons. https://commons.wikimedia.org/wiki/File:Reynisdrangar_01.jpg.

- **West Iceland:** Snæfellsnes Peninsula, nicknamed "Iceland in miniature," boasts Snæfellsjökull volcano, rumored to be the gateway to the underworld. Explore lava fields, geysers, and the dramatic coastline.

Snæfellsjökull volcano.
Kabaeh49, CC BY-SA 3.0 <https://creativecommons.org/licenses/by-sa/3.0>, via Wikimedia Commons. https://commons.wikimedia.org/wiki/File:Snaefellsj%C3%B6kull_von_Rif.jpg

- **Westfjords:** A remote paradise of towering cliffs, hidden fjords, and charming fishing villages like Ísafjörður, untouched by mass tourism and teeming with bird life.

Westfjords.
JavierOlivares, CC BY-SA 4.0 <https://creativecommons.org/licenses/by-sa/4.0>, via Wikimedia Commons. https://commons.wikimedia.org/wiki/File:Vestfir%C3%B0ir,_Westfjords_Icelad.jpg

- **North Iceland**: Mývatn, a volcanic haven of bubbling mud pools and steaming craters. Hike the lunar landscapes of Askja caldera and witness the Dettifoss waterfall, Europe's most picturesque waterfall.

Mývatn.
Arian Zwegers, CC BY 2.0 <https://creativecommons.org/licenses/by/2.0>, via Wikimedia Commons. https://commons.wikimedia.org/wiki/File:M%C3%BDvatn_(6802982523).jpg

- **East Iceland:** Serenity reigns in rolling green hills, glaciers meet the sea, and quaint villages like Seydisfjördur and Djúpivogur exist where time seems to stand still.

Seydisfjördur.
Joe deSousa, CC0, via Wikimedia Commons.
https://commons.wikimedia.org/wiki/File:Sey%C3%B0isfj%C3%B6r%C3%B0ur,_Iceland_(283282 69217).jpg

Volcanoes and Glaciers: A Dance of Fire and Ice

Iceland's heart beats with the primal rhythm of fire and ice. Volcanoes like Hekla and Katla, their slopes cloaked in mystery, stand ready to erupt. On the other hand, glaciers like Vatnajökull, the largest in Europe, carve icy paths through the landscape. Hike the majestic Skaftafell National Park, where glaciers meet the sea, or marvel at the geothermal wonders of the Geysir geothermal area, where Strokkur geyser erupts in an astonishing plume every few minutes.

Waterfalls that Roar, Canyons that Whisper

Iceland's waterfalls are liquid giants, their thunderous roars echoing through valleys. Gullfoss, the Golden Falls, plunges 32 meters in a mesmerizing cascade, while Seljalandsfoss and Skógafoss tumble over cliffs directly into the ocean. Explore hidden gems like Seljalandsfoss's secret passage behind the falls or the dramatic beauty of Svartifoss, its black basalt columns framing the cascading water.

National Parks: Nature's Treasures

Iceland is a treasure trove of national parks, each a haven for nature lovers. Vatnajökull National Park, home to Europe's largest glacier, offers diverse landscapes from volcanic craters to geothermal pools. Skaftafell National Park, with its icy lagoons and black sand beaches, is a photographer's paradise. Thingvellir National Park, a UNESCO World Heritage Site, is where the North American and Eurasian tectonic plates meet, creating dramatic canyons and fissures.

A Map Beyond Borders

This map of majesty extends beyond geographical borders. It weaves together the stories of the people who call this land home. Their resilience is told in ancient sagas, and their creativity is reflected in contemporary art and music. It is a map that invites you to dive deeper, taste the salty spray on your lips, feel the volcanic earth warm your feet, and listen to the whispers of the glaciers.

So, pack your sense of adventure, grab a map (both paper and the one in your heart), and embark on your journey to Iceland. Let the land of fire and ice paint colorful memories with emerald, fiery sunsets and the echo of waterfalls that sing of a land where majesty reigns supreme. Which corner of this majestic land are you most excited to explore?

Iceland through Time: A Journey through Viking Sagas and Modern Sovereignty

Iceland, the Land of Fire and Ice, is more than just a breathtaking compilation of glaciers, volcanoes, and cascading waterfalls. A land where history hums beneath the surface, with tales of Viking settlers, centuries of foreign rule, and a fierce spirit of independence evident in its landscape. Today, you'll journey through Iceland's key historical milestones, exploring the threads that connect its past to its vibrant present.

Viking Roots and Sagas of Old

The story begins in the 9th century, when daring Norse explorers, fleeing Viking raids, set foot on this uncharted island. Led by Ingólfr Arnarson, these pioneers established the first permanent settlement in Reykjavík, laying the foundation for a unique culture steeped in Viking traditions. Sagas, epic prose narratives passed down through generations, became the lifeblood of Icelandic identity. They preserve tales of gods and heroes, mythical creatures, and the harsh realities of life in the unforgiving

North Atlantic.

Centuries of Foreign Rule

Iceland's early years were marked by internal conflicts and attempts to establish a centralized government. The Alþingi, founded in 930, became the world's oldest surviving parliament, a testament to the Icelandic love for democracy. However, the island's isolation and internal struggles led to centuries of foreign rule. From 1262 to 1918, Iceland fell under the dominion of Norway, Denmark, and, briefly, Sweden. This period saw the decline of the Alþingi and the imposition of foreign laws and customs, but it also fueled a growing sense of national identity.

Awakening to Independence

The 19th century witnessed a cultural and political renaissance in Iceland. Jónas Hallgrímsson, a poet and hymn writer, became a national hero for preserving the Icelandic language and literature. The fight for independence gained momentum, culminating in the Act of Union in 1918, which granted Iceland home rule within the Danish kingdom. Finally, in 1944, after years of negotiations, Iceland declared its independence, becoming a republic and charting its course in the world.

Nordic Echoes: A Tapestry of Shared Threads

Iceland's history is intertwined with its Nordic neighbors. The Viking heritage is evident in the Icelandic language, a close relative of Old Norse. It's also visible in cultural traditions like the Jólabústur when the thirteen-troll Yule Lads visit children during the festive season. Architectural influences, seen in the turf-roofed houses and wooden churches, speak of shared Nordic roots. Yet, Iceland's isolation fostered a distinct identity. The sagas, for example, are uniquely Icelandic, reflecting the island's harsh environment and independent spirit.

Modern Iceland: A Beacon of Progress and Creativity

Today, Iceland is a testament to its resilience and unwavering spirit. A modern democracy with a thriving economy, this country ranks high in human development and environmental consciousness. The country's cultural landscape is vibrant, with internationally renowned artists like Björk and Sigur Rós putting Icelandic music on the global map. Iceland's literary tradition continues flourishing, and the Alþingi, a symbol of its long democratic history, remains a cornerstone of its political system.

A Tapestry Unfolding

Iceland's history is a tapestry still being woven; the challenges of climate change and the evolving global landscape demand constant adaptation and innovation. But one thing remains certain: the spirit of the Vikings, the resilience of those first settlers, and the unwavering love for its unique culture and language will continue to guide Iceland's journey through the centuries to come.

So, the next time you gaze upon Iceland's breathtaking landscapes, remember the echoes of its past. Listen to the whispers of the sagas in the wind. See the Viking spirit reflected in the determination of its people.

Beyond Glaciers and Geysers: Unveiling the Heart of Iceland

Iceland captivates you with its otherworldly landscapes and raw natural beauty. However, beneath the volcanic peaks and glacial lagoons lies a vibrant culture. This culture is laden with ancient traditions, quirky customs, and a modern spirit that thrives in the harshest environments. It is time for you to journey beyond the postcards and discover the beating heart of Icelandic life.

- **Warmth in the Land of Ice:** Icelanders, often described as reserved at first, reveal a heart full of warmth and hospitality once you break the ice. Community is paramount, evident in coffee-fueled gatherings and cozy potluck dinners. The annual tradition of Jólabústur is where thirteen mischievous Yule Lads bring gifts (or rotten potatoes!) to children during the thirteen days before Christmas.
- **Traditions Echoing Through Time:** Folklore whispers in the Icelandic wind, shaping customs and celebrations. Belief in elves and hidden people persists, adding a touch of magic to everyday life. Midsummer sees bonfires ablaze, celebrating the longest day of the year, while Thorrablot, a mid-winter feast, honors traditional dishes like smoked puffin and fermented shark (hákarl). These playful and practical customs connect Icelanders to their past and bind them together in the present.
- **Embracing the Untamed:** Icelanders have an innate connection to the wilderness. Hiking volcanic trails, kayaking glacial lagoons, and even swimming in geothermal pools are considered national

pastimes. Respect for nature is ingrained, evident in their commitment to sustainability and environmental protection. This deep connection to the land informs their art, music, and even their sense of humor, often laced with wry observations about the unpredictable weather and the quirks of life in a remote island nation.

Beyond the breathtaking landscapes, Iceland has vibrant traditions, quirky customs, and a fierce spirit that thrives in adversity. Explore the colorful houses huddled beneath volcanic peaks, savor the unique flavors of its cuisine, and lose yourself in the rhythm of its music. You'll discover a warmth that belies the icy exterior, a sense of community forged in shared struggles, and a vibrant ancient and modern culture, a perfect reflection of the Land of Fire and Ice.

A Feast for the Senses in Iceland's Culinary Landscape

Beneath the otherworldly landscapes and raw natural beauty, Iceland captivates you with ancient traditions, modern twists, and flavors that burst with unexpected delight. Grab your fork and settle in, fellow foodie, as you embark on a delicious journey through Iceland's food culture.

From Necessity to Delicacy

Iceland's harsh climate and limited resources have shaped its culinary traditions. Preserving food through drying, fermenting, and smoking became an art form, leading to dishes like hangikjöt (smoked lamb), hakarl (fermented shark), and kleinur (twisted dough pastries). Traditional methods of preserving food – once essential for survival and which impart particular flavors – are now considered delicacies, offering a glimpse into Iceland's past and a testament to its ingenuity.

- **Skyr: Iceland's Yogurt Sensation:** Iceland's gift to the world of breakfast is skyr, a thick, creamy yogurt packed with protein and flavor. More than just a breakfast staple, skyr is a versatile ingredient, appearing in smoothies, desserts, and even savory dishes. Today, skyr has taken the world by storm, with countless variations and flavors gracing supermarket shelves far beyond Iceland's shores.

- **Seafood Bounty:** Surrounded by the icy embrace of the North Atlantic, Iceland's bounty lies in its fresh seafood. Cod, haddock, salmon, and langoustine, the Norway lobster, take center stage, appearing in everything from creamy soups to grilled fillets. Don't miss the chance to try plokkfiskur, a hearty fish stew that warms the soul on a chilly Icelandic day.

- **Lamb with a Viking Flair:** Lamb, a mainstay of Icelandic agriculture, is another culinary hero. Hangikjöt, smoked over birch or sheep dung (yes, you read that right!), is the king of lamb dishes, offering a unique smoky flavor. Lamb is also roasted, grilled, and stewed, each preparation showcasing the rich, tender meat.

- **Modern Reimagination:** Icelandic chefs are not ones to rest on their laurels. They infuse traditional flavors with global influences, creating innovative dishes that delight. Michelin-starred restaurants like Dill offer Nordic cuisine with a twist, while local cafes and bistros tempt with modern takes on classic comfort food.

- **Beyond the Plate:** No Icelandic culinary experience is complete without a taste of brennivín, the national schnapps distilled from caraway seeds. Often paired with hákarl for a true test of your palate, brennivín has a warming kick and a distinct, licorice-like flavor. Coffee, too, is a national obsession, fueling late-night conversations and keeping spirits high during the long winter months.

- **Sweet Treats for a Cold Climate:** Icelanders have a sweet tooth, and their desserts reflect their ingenuity. Kleinur, those twisted dough pastries, are often enjoyed with coffee or as a mid-afternoon treat. With its creamy sweetness, panna cotta is a popular choice, while vínarterta, a traditional layer cake soaked in wine, is a decadent treat for special occasions.

- **A Culinary Adventure Awaits:** So, come hungry, come curious, and come ready to be surprised by the flavors of Iceland. From traditional dishes steeped in history to modern culinary creations, Iceland's food scene offers an unforgettable experience for your taste buds. Whether you're braving a bite of hákarl or savoring a perfectly grilled langoustine, remember, food is a window into a culture, and Iceland's culinary landscape is a story waiting to be tasted.

Don't be afraid to try new things! Ask locals for recommendations, visit food markets, and sample traditional dishes. You might discover a new favorite food in the Land of Fire and Ice.

A Journey through Iceland's Creative Pulse

Iceland has a heart that expresses itself in a combination of art, literature, music, and creative expressions as unique as the island itself. It's time to explore this mix of creativity, where nature's drama collides with human imagination, shaping a distinct Icelandic identity.

- **Art that Mirrors the Landscape:** Nature is the muse for Icelandic art in all its untamed glory. Bold strokes by Jóhannes Kjarval capture the volcanic fury of mountains, while Erró's surreal landscapes echo the island's unpredictable weather. Contemporary artists like Kristín Jónsdóttir breathe life into recycled materials, reflecting the islanders' resilience and resourcefulness. From lava rock sculptures to glacial ice installations, nature is not just scenery but a living participant in the artistic dialogue.
- **Sagas Whispering in the Wind:** Iceland's literary heritage is as ancient as its glaciers. The sagas, epic tales passed down through generations, tell of Viking history, mythical creatures, and the harsh realities of life on the island. These narratives have inspired contemporary writers like Halldór Laxness, a Nobel Prize laureate, who explores themes of isolation, faith, and the human spirit in the face of unforgiving landscapes. Today, a new generation of writers weave contemporary stories, tackling social issues and everyday life with wit and insight.
- **Music that Dances with the Elements:** You hear the wind whistling through fjords, the thunder of waterfalls, and the rhythmic rumble of volcanoes forming the foundation of Icelandic music. Sigur Rós' melancholic melodies echo the desolate beauty of glacial plains, while Björk's electronic beats pulsate with the volcanic energy of the earth. Bands such as Of Monsters and Men and Kaleo fuse folk traditions with modern rock, creating a haunting and energetic sound. Music festivals like Secret Solstice and Iceland Airwaves pulsate with life, celebrating the island's vibrant musical landscape.
- **Beyond the Big Canvas:** Creative expression is seen everywhere. Fashion designers translate the island's stark beauty into bold,

textured garments. Culinary art elevates fresh seafood and local ingredients to Michelin-starred masterpieces. Street art murals add color to urban landscapes, reflecting social commentary and everyday humor. Even the annual sheep round-up becomes a spectacle, transforming a vibrant cultural event with music, storytelling, and community spirit.

- **Grit and Beauty:** Icelandic art, literature, music, and creative expressions are more than just entertainment. They are reflections of the soul of the nation. They embody the resilience forged in centuries of battling harsh weather and isolation, the quiet humor that emerges in the face of adversity, and the deep connection to the raw beauty of their land. Each brushstroke, every chord, and every word whispers a story of the human spirit woven into a tapestry as dynamic and ever-changing as the Land of Fire and Ice.

Immerse yourself in Iceland's creative spirit. Visit art galleries, attend a concert, or pick up a local novel. Learn a few Icelandic phrases to appreciate the lyrics of their music. Remember, art is a conversation, so engage with Iceland's creative voice. You might discover a new perspective on this extraordinary island.

Iceland's Wild Ride: Choosing Your Transatlantic Chariot

Iceland beckons with its otherworldly landscapes, but navigating its vast expanses can feel like deciphering an ancient Viking riddle. Fear not, intrepid traveler. This guide reveals the diverse transportation options in Iceland, helping you choose the chariot that suits your adventure.

Hitting the Open Road:

- **Rental Cars:** The ultimate symbol of freedom, renting a car offers flexibility and independence. Explore hidden corners, stop on a whim for breathtaking photo ops, and blast Björk on the stereo like nobody's watching. Just be prepared for gravel roads, unpredictable weather, and the occasional sheep crossing (they have the right of way!).
- **Buses and Shuttles:** For budget-conscious adventurers, Iceland's extensive bus network connects major towns and popular attractions. Hop on a hop-off tour or between villages, enjoying

the scenery and meeting fellow travelers. Be mindful of limited schedules and pre-book for high-season travel.
- **Super Jeeps:** These rugged beasts conquer glaciers, mountains, and volcanic trails inaccessible to regular vehicles. Join a guided super jeep tour to traverse hidden landscapes, explore hidden waterfalls, and feel the thrill of off-road adventure.

Taking Flight:
- **Domestic Flights:** Domestic flights offer speedy connections for travelers short on time or wanting to reach remote corners. Soar over glacial valleys, marvel at volcanic peaks from above, and land in charming villages accessible only by air. Keep in mind the higher cost compared to ground transportation.
- **Helicopter Tours:** Treat yourself to the ultimate bird's-eye view of Iceland's dramatic beauty. Explore active volcanoes, land on glacier ice caps, or witness the midnight sun from a private helicopter tour. Prepare for a hefty price tag, but the memories will be priceless.

Sailing the Seas:
- **Boat Tours:** Take a different perspective on Iceland by exploring its stunning coastline and fjords by boat. Witness soaring cliffs, spot playful puffins, or cruise between icebergs in Jökulsárlón glacial lagoon. Choose from whale-watching tours, day trips, or even multi-day sailing adventures.

Off the Beaten Path:
- **Hiking and Cycling:** Enjoy the landscape on foot or two wheels. Hike iconic trails like Laugavegurinn or explore hidden valleys by bike. Embrace the fresh air, the scenery, and the sense of accomplishment. Remember, proper gear and planning are essential in Iceland's unpredictable weather.
- **Horseback Riding:** Experience Iceland like the Vikings did with a horseback riding tour. Gallop across black sand beaches, traverse geothermal fields, and feel the rhythm of the land beneath you. Choose from gentle trail rides to exhilarating gallops, suitable for all levels.

Tips for Choosing Your Chariot:
- **Budget:** Factor in costs, comparing rental car mileage vs. bus fares or splurging on a once-in-a-lifetime helicopter tour.

- **Time:** Choose a mode that matches your itinerary, balancing scenic road trips with faster flights for remote destinations.
- **Interests:** Hikers and photographers may prefer flexibility, while adrenaline junkies will crave super jeeps or glacier expeditions.
- **Accessibility:** Consider if mobility limitations require specific options like automatic cars or boat tours with wheelchair access.

Remember, the journey is just as important as the destination in Iceland. Download travel apps like Maps.me and 112 Iceland for offline navigation and emergency assistance. Research road conditions and weather forecasts before embarking on your journey. So, choose your chariot wisely, embrace the adventure, and let Iceland's wild beauty carry you away.

Quirks and Curiosities of the Land of Fire and Ice

Iceland will captivate your imagination with its breathtaking landscapes and raw natural beauty. Iceland is a land teeming with quirky customs, unexpected delights, and fascinating facts that make it truly unique. So, buckle up, fellow adventurer. Here's a sneak peek into Iceland's offbeat side.

1. **Elves Among Us:** Believe it or not, a significant portion of Icelanders believe in elves, the hidden people dwelling in rocks, mountains, and waterfalls. Don't be surprised if you encounter elf houses sprinkled throughout the countryside, built with reverence for these mythical creatures.
2. **Hot Dogs (Seriously):** Forget fancy Michelin-starred meals. Icelanders' true street food love affair lies with hot dogs. These aren't your average variety, however. Topped with rémoulade sauce, crispy fried onions, and raw onions, they're a national obsession, devoured at late-night stands and on the go. Be warned, though, that one might not be enough.
3. **Beer Banned and Then Boomed:** From 1915 to 1989, beer was a forbidden fruit in Iceland. This bizarre ban arose from concerns about alcoholism and economic stability. After years of clandestine brews and whispered jokes, the dam finally broke in 1989. Today, Iceland boasts a thriving craft beer scene, brewing delicious ales to quench the thirst of liberated

beer lovers.

4. **Shark for the Brave:** Hákarl, *fermented shark*, is not for the faint of heart. This traditional Icelandic dish is made from Greenland Shark – which is poisonous when fresh. If you're feeling adventurous, try a tiny piece with a shot of Brennivín (Icelandic schnapps) to chase away the lingering sensations.

5. **Midnight Sun and Northern Lights:** Iceland offers a front-row seat to two celestial spectacles. In summer, experience the surreal beauty of the midnight sun, where daylight stretches into the wee hours. During winter, witness the aurora borealis paint the night sky with mesmerizing dances of green, purple, and red lights.

6. **Volcanic Namesakes:** In Iceland, where fire and ice reign supreme, even names reflect the landscape. Geysers are often named after their discoverers, with Strokkur ("Churn") and Geysir ("Gusher") living up to their monikers. Volcanoes, too, have evocative names like Hekla ("Cloak") and Katla ("Caldera").

Pack an Icelandic phrasebook, embrace the unexpected, and be prepared for the occasional volcanic eruption (figurative and literal!). Iceland, with its quirks and charms, awaits your adventurous spirit. Come with an open mind and a sense of humor, and let the Land of Fire and Ice surprise you with its unexpected delights. You will leave with a story (or two) to tell.

Chapter 2: To and From the Airport

Landing at Keflavík International Airport (KEF), Iceland's international gateway, marks the beginning of your Icelandic adventure. However, before you embark on your glacier hikes, geothermal dips, and puffin-spotting expeditions, you'll have to navigate the airport and choose the perfect transport to your destination. Worry not, intrepid traveler, for this chapter is your compass!

Keflavík International Airport.
Jeff Hitchcock from Seattle, WA, USA, CC BY 2.0 <https://creativecommons.org/licenses/by/2.0>, via Wikimedia Commons.
https://commons.wikimedia.org/wiki/File:Keflav%C3%ADk_International_Airport_(31001876723).jpg

A Compass for Iceland's Airport Labyrinth

The wheels touch down in Keflavík, Iceland's gateway to geothermal wonders and endless adventure. But before the Northern Lights dance in your vision, an immediate hurdle arises. You must conquer Keflavík International Airport's (KEF) transportation labyrinth. Fear not, intrepid traveler, for a veritable smorgasbord of options awaits, ready to whisk you to your Icelandic odyssey. Whether you're a budget backpacker scaling glaciers or a luxury seeker soaking in geothermal lagoons, this section will equip you to navigate Keflavík's transit hub with ease, transforming your arrival into a seamless extension of your Icelandic experience.

Soaring Above the Land of Fire and Ice

If your destination lies in Iceland's interior, domestic flights offer a breathtaking alternative. You'll be skimming over volcanic peaks and glacial tongues, Akureyri's fjords glittering in the distance, or Ísafjörður's colorful houses clinging to dramatic cliffs. Air Iceland Connect and Eagle Air weave their wings across the island, so check their schedules and prepare to be awestruck by the aerial tapestry of this unique land.

Your Guide to Smoother Icelandic Transitions

As your plane touches down at Iceland's Keflavík International Airport, KEF for short, finding your way can feel like a cryptic puzzle. It's time to tackle this immediate hurdle.

- **Navigating the Arrival Hall:** From baggage claim to currency exchange, KEF's arrival hall is well-organized. Look for clear signage directing you to your next step, whether it's immigration, customs, or baggage collection. Helpful staff are always on hand to answer questions, so don't hesitate to ask if you're unsure.

- **Fueling up for Exploration:** Icelandic cuisine awaits. Grab a quick bite at the arrival hall food court, which offers Icelandic street food and global favorites. For a sit-down experience, Lava Restaurant and Kaffi Duus offer stunning views and delicious meals. Remember, Icelandic supermarkets also offer tasty and healthy options to fuel your adventures.

- **Beyond Reykjavík:** Iceland's magic extends far beyond the capital. Buses and domestic flights connect KEF with major towns and villages across the island, from Akureyri's northern charm to Vík í Mýrdal's black sand beaches. Check timetables online or at the airport information desk to plan your onward journey.

Green Choices: Traveling with Mother Nature in Mind

As you navigate Keflavík's transport options, remember that environmentally conscious choices are always welcome. Strætó buses and Airport Direct operate with an eye on fuel efficiency, while electric car rentals are increasingly common. Moreover, some tour companies offer carbon offsetting programs, allowing you to minimize the environmental impact of your journey. Consider these options and feel the satisfaction of traveling in harmony with Iceland's breathtaking landscapes.

Connecting to the World: Staying Wired in the Land of Sagas

Iceland pulsates with digital connectivity, ensuring you stay in touch with the world regardless of how remote your adventure is. Keflavík Airport provides free Wi-Fi throughout the terminal, and most buses and rental cars offer in-vehicle options. Prepaid SIM cards or data roaming packages from your phone provider keep you connected, allowing you to share Icelandic magic with loved ones back home. Disconnecting and immersing yourself in the present moment is equally rewarding in this land of natural wonders.

Essential Services

- **Currency Exchange:** ATMs and currency exchange desks are readily available in the arrival hall and throughout the airport. Remember to check your bank's fees before withdrawing cash.
- **Luggage Storage:** Need to store your bags for a day trip or overnight stay? Luggage storage facilities are available at the airport, offering secure and convenient options.
- **Information Desks:** Friendly staff at the Information Desks are happy to answer any questions about the airport, transportation options, or local services.
- **Duty-Free Shopping:** Before your departure, indulge in Icelandic souvenirs and gourmet treats at the duty-free shops. Remember, duty-free allowances apply, so check with customs before indulging.

Local Tips:

- Download the Klappið app for easy and affordable public transport ticketing.
- Purchase a prepaid SIM card for convenient mobile internet access throughout your trip.

- Consider carbon offsetting programs to minimize your environmental impact.
- Pack warm layers and waterproof gear, even in summer, as Icelandic weather can be unpredictable.
- Most importantly, relax and embrace the adventure. Iceland's magic unfolds at its own pace, so let go of the schedule and enjoy the journey.

Bus Bonanza: From Budget Blitzkrieg to Comfort Cruisers:
- **Flybus:** The reigning champion of convenience, Flybus operates with the precision of a Swiss watch, its bright blue chariots whisking you directly to Reykjavík's heart or select hotels. There's no need to battle jet lag or decipher schedules. Step off the plane, hop on the bus, and arrive refreshed in the midst of the city's vibrant pulse. Tickets are readily available online or at kiosks in the arrival hall, making Flybus a stress-free choice for even the weariest traveler.
- **Airport Direct:** Offering similar speed and comfort, Airport Direct takes a slightly different approach. Instead of dropping you at your hotel, it stops at the terminal before hurtling towards Reykjavík. This budget-friendly option is ideal for solo travelers or those who don't mind a short extra hop to their destination. Tickets can be secured online or at their terminal counter, ensuring a smooth transition from arrival to exploration.
- **Strætó Public Bus:** The local hero, Strætó bs, champions affordability and accessibility. Route 55, a 24/7 workhorse, takes you straight to BSÍ Bus Terminal, Reykjavík's transportation hub, while other routes connect Keflavík with surrounding villages like Keflavík town and Grindavík. Download the Strætó app or gather your exact change and hop aboard for an authentic Icelandic experience amidst locals heading home or embarking on their adventures.

Expanding Your Icelandic Horizons

Iceland's magic extends far beyond Reykjavík's embrace. Buses connect Keflavík with major towns and villages across the island. Check timetables on websites like Straeto.is or Iceland Excursions, and let the diverse tapestry of Icelandic landscapes unfurl before you. For remote destinations, domestic flights or private transfers offer the fastest access, ensuring you reach your desired corner of paradise without delay.

Navigating Beyond Keflavík: Charting Your Course through Iceland

Once you've arrived at your destination, exploring Iceland's diverse landscapes unfolds like an open book. Public buses connect major towns and villages, while local car rentals grant ultimate flexibility. For breathtaking treks and off-the-beaten-path adventures, guided tours with experienced locals offer invaluable insights and safety. Don't forget to download maps and navigation apps. Sometimes, the most rewarding discoveries happen when you simply wander and let the landscape guide you.

Taxi Time: Speed and Luxury for the Discerning Traveler

For those who value time and comfort, taxis are found outside the terminal, ready to whisk you away in a cocoon of leather and air conditioning. While pricier than other options, they offer flexibility and convenience, especially for late arrivals or groups with luggage in tow. Don't hesitate to ask for an estimate before setting off, and if Uber beckons, its app-based magic operates in Iceland, too.

Rental Rendezvous: Iceland on Your Terms

Iceland begs to be explored at your own pace, and what better way than behind the wheel? Car rental companies line up at Keflavík, offering many vehicles to match your budget and itinerary. From fuel-efficient hatchbacks to rugged jeeps, Iceland's open roads await. Remember, driving requires careful planning, especially during winter, so check road conditions and follow the local rules before embarking on your four-wheeled adventure.

Private Tours: Tailored Tranquility from Touchdown to Adventure

Craving a curated experience from the moment you land? Private transfers cater to your specific desires, delivering you directly to your accommodation or the starting point of your chosen adventure. Whether it's a glacier hike or a soak in the Blue Lagoon, tour companies weave your airport transfer into the fabric of your Icelandic vacation, ensuring a seamless transition from arrival to exploration.

Unveiling Iceland's Regional Airport Treasures

Iceland's allure extends far beyond the vibrant pulse of Reykjavík. Its windswept landscapes, dramatic fjords, and geothermal wonders beckon from every corner, each whispering tales of adventure and untamed beauty. To discover these hidden gems, venturing beyond the bustling capital is vital, and a network of regional airports awaits as your gateway to the Icelandic soul.

- **Akureyri Airport (AEY):** The "capital of the North," Akureyri basks in the embrace of Eyjafjörður fjord, a haven for outdoor enthusiasts. From AEY, the majestic Goðafoss waterfall roars its welcome, inviting you to explore verdant valleys and volcanic plateaus. Hike the otherworldly landscapes of Lake Mývatn, where geothermal springs bubble and fumaroles hiss. Akureyri offers convenient connections to Reykjavík, Egilsstaðir, and Þórshöfn, making it a strategic base for weaving North Iceland's magic into your Icelandic tapestry.

- **Egilsstaðir Airport (EGS):** The rugged Eastfjords rise like stoic sentinels on the eastern coast, beckoning those seeking raw, untamed beauty. EGS opens the door to this dramatic playground, where cascading waterfalls carve through moss-carpeted cliffs and quaint fishing villages cling to fjord-kissed shores. Venture into Skaftafell National Park, where glaciers carve icy paths and the Jökulsárlón lagoon shimmers with diamond-like icebergs. From EGS, domestic flights to Reykjavík and Akureyri make it easy to combine East Iceland's wild spirit with the charm of the North.

- **Ísafjörður Airport (IFJ):** Carved into the heart of the Westfjords, IFJ serves as a portal to a world where time seems to stand still. Here, amidst fjord-carved coves and snow-capped peaks, remote villages whisper tales of a simpler life. Lace up your hiking boots and trek through pristine valleys, kayak through shimmering fjords, or stand transfixed beneath the Aurora Borealis' celestial dance. IFJ primarily offers connections to Reykjavík, but for those seeking the soul of the Westfjords, its isolation becomes a badge of honor.

- **Hornafjörður Airport (HFN):** Nestled beneath the shadow of Vatnajökull, Europe's largest glacier, HFN unlocks the secrets of Southeast Iceland. From this small airport, a world of glacial grandeur unfolds. Witness the ethereal beauty of Jökulsárlón glacier lagoon, where icebergs drift on a turquoise canvas, or embark on a boat tour amidst these glittering giants. HFN's domestic flights to Reykjavík make it an enchanting starting point for your Southeast Iceland adventure.

- **Vestmannaeyjar Airport (VEY)**: For a truly unique Icelandic experience, VEY whisks you away to the Westman Islands, a volcanic archipelago teeming with life. Hike the Eldfell volcano, a testament to fiery forces, explore lava caves carved by molten whispers, and witness the comical waddle of adorable puffins. VEY's domestic flights to Reykjavík make the islands a perfect day trip or a charming base for your Westmannaeyjar adventure.
- **Húsavík Airport (HZK)**: HZK, nestled in Iceland's "whale watching capital," beckons adventure seekers to its pristine shores. From this charming town, set sail amongst giants, witnessing humpback whales breaching and minke whales gliding through icy waters. The thrill of encountering these magnificent creatures in their natural habitat is an experience that will be forever etched in your memory. HZK's domestic flights to Reykjavík make Húsavík a convenient stop on your North Iceland expedition.

These regional airports are not just stepping stones; they are the keys to unlocking Iceland's diverse treasures. Each location boasts its unique charm, offering a gateway to untouched landscapes, vibrant local cultures, and experiences that will forever resonate within you. So, ditch the well-worn tourist trail, embrace the whispers of the wind, and let these regional airports guide you to your Icelandic odyssey.

Beyond the airport door, a plethora of transportation options await. Rent a car for the ultimate freedom, hop on a local bus and connect with the rhythm of daily life, or indulge in a guided tour for curated adventure. Each journey unfolds like a personal saga, waiting to be written on the canvas of the Icelandic wilderness.

Plan your exploration, book your flights with anticipation, and pack your spirit of adventure. As you step off the plane and breathe in the crisp Icelandic air, remember the journey is just as important as the destination. Embrace the slower pace, savor the unexpected encounters, and let the whispers of the regional airports lead you to your corner of Icelandic paradise.

Leaving Iceland with a Heartbeat Echoing Volcanoes

As your Icelandic odyssey nears its bittersweet finale, the air crackles with a poignant blend of farewell and anticipation. The Northern Lights, once guiding stars on your arrival, now bid you farewell on your departure with celestial brushstrokes. Keflavík Airport, the portal that ushered you into this land of fire and ice, transforms into a stage for your final act. You'll discover farewell options as diverse as the landscapes you traversed.

Retracing the Footsteps of Wonder

For some, leaving Iceland means reliving the magic of arrival. Hop aboard the familiar chariot of Flybus or Airport Direct, retracing the path that led you to Reykjavík's vibrant pulse. Let the cityscape unfold like a memory reel, each landmark a whispered echo of laughter shared with newfound friends, the thrill of hikes through lunar landscapes, and the awe-inspiring serenity of geothermal pools. Breathe in the crisp air, tinged with bittersweet nostalgia, and let the familiar sights and sounds weave a final embrace of the Icelandic magic that touched your soul.

Embarking on Untrodden Paths

Perhaps your heart yearns for one last unexplored adventure. Ditch the familiar and opt for a Strætó bus, venturing beyond Reykjavík's embrace. Wind your way through charming villages, each house's colorful facade reflecting the warmth of Icelandic hospitality. Or, rent a car for one last hurrah, chasing the setting sun down deserted coastline roads. Let the wind whisper secrets of ancient sagas in your ear as you carve your path through this land of endless possibility. Transform your departure into an unexpected continuation, a final act filled with the thrill of discovery and whispered farewells to landscapes you may never see again.

Indulging in a Farewell Fit for Valkyries

For those who crave a touch of grandeur in their goodbyes, Iceland offers a myriad of luxurious experiences. Sink into the plush comfort of a private transfer, Iceland's breathtaking landscapes gliding past your window like a cinematic farewell film. Imagine a stop at a secluded geothermal pool, where steaming waters soothe your soul and volcanic whispers echo in the air. Raise a final toast with panoramic views of glaciers and waterfalls, a fitting finale to the tapestry of your Icelandic memories.

Savoring the Last Bites of Paradise

Keflavík Airport is far from a sterile goodbye zone and a treasure trove of final Icelandic delights. Explore the duty-free shops, a wonderland of volcanic beauty products, hand-knitted woolen wonders, and gourmet treats that capture the essence of Iceland's bounty. Pamper your taste buds at Kaffi Duus, where the aroma of freshly baked pastries mingles with panoramic views of the Icelandic sky. Let each bite be a savoring of the island's flavors, a final Icelandic indulgence warming your soul as you prepare to embark on your journey home.

Whispering Farewells Beneath the Earth's Heartbeat

If time allows, weave one final magic thread into your Icelandic tapestry. Journey beneath the Blue Lagoon, where the Lava Tunnel Raufarhólshellir beckons. Walk through volcanic veins carved by fiery whispers, the earth's ancient heartbeat echoing in the cool darkness. Witness the raw power and enduring beauty of this land of fire and ice, a fitting final chapter that leaves you breathless with awe. This surreal experience becomes a whispered farewell, a reminder that Iceland's magic lives on, not just in the landscapes you see but in the memories you carry within.

As you board your plane, Iceland's magic is still shimmering in your eyes. The memories woven into the fabric of your being are your eternal souvenirs. It's the passport to Iceland within you, a place you can return to in the quiet moments, savoring every thread of your adventure under the starlight.

Remember, your departure is not an ending but a bridge to a future longing. It's the start of a lifelong love affair with Iceland, a yearning for the windswept landscapes, the smell of freshly brewed coffee, and the whispers of ancient sagas. Let your goodbye be a promise to return, a vow to weave yourself back into this tapestry of fire and ice.

With this guide as your compass, navigating Keflavík's transportation maze becomes a breeze. Whether you prioritize speed, budget, or eco-conscious travel, Iceland offers options to meet your every need. So, embrace the adventure, choose your path, and allow Keflavík to be the gateway to an unforgettable Icelandic odyssey. Remember, the journey is just as important as the destination, so enjoy every twist and turn as you conquer the Keflavík labyrinth and embark on your Icelandic dream.

Chapter 3: Reykjavík: The Capital

Reykjavík, Iceland's vibrant capital, is where Viking lore collides with neon lights, and steaming geothermal vents whisper tales of fiery creation. The city's cafes hum with the infectious energy of a nation pulsating with modern art and ancient sagas. In this chapter, you'll crack open the heart of Reykjavík, traversing through its cobbled streets and graffiti-laced alleyways, revealing its hidden gems and dazzling landmarks.

Whether you're a history buff yearning to trace the footsteps of Norse gods, a culture vulture seeking the heartbeat of Iceland's creative scene, or an adventure seeker craving glacial winds in your hair, Reykjavík promises an unforgettable symphony of experiences.

Reykjavík

OpenStreetMap contributors, CC BY-SA 2.0 <https://creativecommons.org/licenses/by-sa/2.0>, via Wikimedia Commons https://commons.wikimedia.org/wiki/File:OSM_Mapnik_Reykjav%C3%ADk_2019-03-29.png

Historical Background

Reykjavík, Iceland's vibrant capital, pulsates with a life force as unique as the island itself. This city, cradled against the backdrop of snow-capped peaks and geothermal wonders, wears its history on its sleeve – each quaint street and iconic landmark weaving a tale of fiery creation, Viking sagas, and modern revolution. To truly understand Reykjavík is to delve into its rich tapestry, tracing the threads of its past that form the vibrant fabric of the present.

From Smoked Bay to Bustling Capital

Reykjavík's name, meaning "Bay of Smokes," hints at its fiery origins. Founded in 874 AD by Ingólfur Arnarson, a Norse chieftain lured by geothermal springs and fish-rich waters, the city's early years were humble. Houses huddled in lava fields, smoke from turf roofs painting the sky with wispy trails. Life revolved around fishing, with a smattering of sheep farming and trade. For centuries, Reykjavík remained a sleepy village, its fortunes fluctuating with the winds of Icelandic politics and natural disasters.

A Century of Transformation

The 19th century ushered in a seismic shift. As trade flourished, Reykjavík shed its rural skin, morphing into a bustling town. The Alþingi, Iceland's ancient parliament, relocated here in 1843, solidifying Reykjavík's role as the island's cultural and political heart. Houses grew taller, streets sprouted cobblestones, and a surge of artistic and intellectual energy pulsed through the newly-defined capital.

Modernity Takes Root

The 20th century saw Iceland break free from Danish rule, and Reykjavík embraced its newfound independence with gusto. Modern buildings graced the skyline, reflecting a nation yearning for progress. From the striking Harpa Concert Hall, its glass facade shimmering like an aurora borealis, to the soaring Hallgrímskirkja church, its steeple piercing the skies, Reykjavík abounds with contemporary Icelandic design.

A Tapestry Woven by Nature

Reykjavík hasn't forgotten its fiery roots; geothermal energy hums beneath every street, visible in steaming vents and pools of turquoise water. Wild winds whip through streets, carrying the scent of the North Atlantic. Even within the city limits, nature holds sway, with parks and trails offering escapes into the embrace of rolling hills and volcanic terrain.

Understanding the City's Layout

Reykjavík, home to charming cafes and graceful swans, unfolds like a vibrant fan, its streets radiating outwards from the picturesque Lake Tjörnin. With its colorful houses and eclectic shops, the Old Town sits at the heart of the city, a maze of cobbled streets whispering tales of bygone eras. Laugavegur, the city's main artery, pulsates with energy and is lined with cafes, bars, and design boutiques. Newer districts like 101 Reykjavik and Grandi Harbor offer stylish accommodations and trendy restaurants.

Reykjavík Today

Today, Reykjavík stands as a testament to Iceland's spirit. A city where Viking sagas mingle with modern art, geothermal heat warms the streets, and the Northern Lights paint the sky with celestial brushstrokes. A vibrant mosaic of history, culture, and natural beauty, the city beckons travelers to explore its depths and create their Icelandic odyssey.

So, walk into the streets of Reykjavík, let the whispers of its history guide you, and discover the vibrant tapestry woven from fire, ice, and the indomitable spirit of a nation.

Did You Know: Reykjavík is the world's northernmost capital city, located further north than even Anchorage, Alaska. Despite its compact size, it pulsates with the cultural heart of Iceland.

Main Attractions

Reykjavík, Iceland's vibrant capital, is a city where the pulse of history and modern marvels intertwine. From soaring churches that pierce the sky to shimmering concert halls that sing with the harmony of light and glass, Reykjavík's landmarks are more than just tourist magnets; they are portals to the soul of this unique island nation. So, pack your sense of wonder and prepare to be dazzled by these must-see attractions:

Hallgrímskirkja: A Beacon of Faith and Skyline Star

Hallgrímskirkja church.

Yosleisyvaldes, CC BY-SA 4.0 <https://creativecommons.org/licenses/by-sa/4.0>, via Wikimedia Commons: https://commons.wikimedia.org/wiki/File:Hallgr%C3%ADmskirkja,_church_of_Hallgr%C3%ADmur.jpg

Rising above the city like a sentinel bathed in midnight sunlight, Hallgrímskirkja church is Reykjavík's undeniable landmark. Inspired by Icelandic basalt columns, its colossal concrete frame dominates the skyline. Climb the tower for panoramic views that stretch from the city's heart to the snow-capped peaks beyond. Inside, lose yourself in the ethereal play of light and shadow cast by the vast stained glass windows and marvel at the 5,275-pipe organ, one of the largest in Iceland.

As of the writing of this book, the normal opening hours for the Church are Sunday to Saturday from 9 AM to 8 PM and the Tower is open on the same days from 10 AM to 4:45 PM, but please double-check the opening hours online should there have been any slight change in their schedule.

Harpa: Where Music Meets Magic

Inside the Harpa concert Hall
https://www.rawpixel.com/image/6019600/photo-image-public-domain-glass-window

Harpa Concert Hall, a jewel shimmering on Reykjavík's waterfront, is a testament to Iceland's artistic spirit. Its honeycomb-like facade, sculpted by light and reflections, echoes the frozen beauty of glacial icebergs. Step inside and be transported to a world of acoustic wonder, where the sounds of orchestras and avant-garde performances dance in the air. Attend a concert, explore the exhibitions, or bask in the architectural brilliance of this modern masterpiece.

As of the writing of this book, the normal opening hours are every day of the week from 10 AM to 6 PM, but please double-check the opening hours online should there have been any slight change in their schedule.

Perlan: A Panoramic Playground on a Volcanic Wonder

Perlan viewing deck.
Xfigpower, CC BY-SA 3.0 <https://creativecommons.org/licenses/by-sa/3.0>, via Wikimedia Commons: https://commons.wikimedia.org/wiki/File:View_from_Perlan_Viewing_Deck_(2).jpg

Perlan, perched atop Reykjavík's iconic water tanks, is more than just a restaurant. It's a multi-sensory experience that lets you explore Iceland's wonders in miniature. Take a rotating ride to the observation deck for 360-degree views of the city and its breathtaking surroundings. Walk through the immersive glacier exhibition, feel the earth tremble in the simulated earthquake, and marvel at the Northern Lights projected on the dome ceiling. Perlan is a reminder that even in the heart of the city, the magic of Iceland's natural beauty is never far away.

As of the writing of this book, the normal opening hours are every day from 9 AM to 10 PM, but please double-check the opening hours online should there have been any slight change in their schedule.

Sun Voyager: A Steel Dream Chasing Horizons

Standing proudly on the Reykjavík shoreline, the Sun Voyager symbolizes Iceland's yearning for endless daylight and uncharted territories. This sleek, metallic sculpture, designed by Einar Jónsson, captures the essence of a Viking ship slicing through the waves, its prow forever pointed toward the horizon. Take a walk along the pier, feel the spray of the ocean on your face, and let the Sun Voyager inspire your dreams of adventure.

As of the writing of this book, the Sun Voyager is open 24 hours a day, seven days a week, but please double-check the opening hours online should there have been any slight change in their schedule.

Beyond the Big Names: Hidden Gems Await

While these landmarks are undeniable highlights, Reykjavík's charm lies in its hidden corners and unexpected delights. Explore the quirky street art that adorns buildings, discover the treasures of Laugavegur's independent shops, or lose yourself in the vibrant chaos of the Kolaportið flea market. Take a boat tour to the tiny island of Viðey, a haven for puffins and historical ruins, or wander through the peaceful oasis of Grótta lighthouse, where the ocean whispers tales of shipwrecks and ancient sagas.

Reykjavík's landmarks are more than just sightseeing stops. They're invitations to unravel the city's layers of history, culture, and natural wonder. So, let these landmarks be your guide. Don't forget to stray from the beaten path and discover the magic that lies hidden in every corner of this captivating city. Remember, Reykjavík's true beauty lies in the stories its landmarks whisper and the connections you forge with its vibrant spirit.

Did You Know: The area where Reykjavík now stands was once a humble sheep farm. Ingólfur Arnarson, Iceland's first permanent settler, stumbled upon the geothermal springs and abundant fish around 874 AD, leading to the city's birth.

Transport

Reykjavík, Iceland's vibrant capital, beckons with its charming streets, geothermal wonders, and breathtaking landscapes. However, before you embark on your Icelandic odyssey, mastering the art of getting around is key. This section will equip you with the knowledge and confidence to navigate Reykjavík like a seasoned local, whether you prefer the convenience of public transportation, the thrill of two wheels, or the freedom of the open road.

Hopping on the Strætó

Reykjavík's public bus system, Strætó, is your budget-friendly champion. Download the Strætó app to purchase tickets and plan your journey. With a network of buses crisscrossing the city, reaching your destination is a breeze. Hop on and off at designated stops, explore diverse neighborhoods, and soak up the local vibe. Remember, validate your ticket upon boarding and consider purchasing a multi-day pass for significant savings.

Taxi Tales

For speed and convenience, taxis are your go-to. While pricier than Strætó, they're ideal for late-night adventures, luggage-laden journeys, or simply arriving in style. Pre-booking online or calling a taxi company in advance will save you time and money. Remember, tipping is not mandatory but always appreciated.

Pedal Power

Embrace the fresh air and scenic views with Reykjavík's extensive network of bike paths. Rent a bike from one of the numerous rental shops and explore the city at your own pace. Cruise along the waterfront, meander through charming streets, or conquer Mount Esja for panoramic rewards. Just remember to follow the traffic rules and wear a helmet for safety.

Walking Wonders

Reykjavík is a compact city, perfectly suited for exploration on foot. Lace up your walking shoes and discover hidden gems around every corner. Stroll along Laugavegur, Reykjavík's main artery, and browse through quirky shops. Wander through the Old Town, where colorful houses whisper tales of the past. Or take a scenic walk along the Sólheimasandur Plane Wreck, where a black sand beach cradles a DC-3 plane, a surreal reminder of Iceland's rugged beauty.

Car Rentals

For those seeking independence and the freedom to explore beyond city limits, car rental offers the ultimate flexibility. Rent a car and venture into the Golden Circle, marvel at the cascading Gullfoss waterfall, or drive along the scenic South Coast, where glaciers, waterfalls, and black sand beaches paint a dramatic landscape. However, factor in car rental costs, parking fees, and Icelandic driving conditions before taking the wheel.

Beyond Reykjavík

Public buses connect Reykjavík to nearby towns and villages, allowing you to explore Akureyri in the north, Vík í Mýrdal in the south, or the charming fishing village of Grindavík. For longer distances, domestic flights offer quick connections to other regions.

Essential Tips:
- Purchase the Reykjavík City Card for discounted public transportation, free museum entry, and other perks.
- Validate your ticket upon boarding Strætó buses.
- Taxis are readily available at taxi ranks or on-call.
- Download offline maps and essential apps like Strætó and Google Translate for navigation.
- Be mindful of weather conditions and dress accordingly.
- Respect Icelandic traffic rules and road etiquette.

The best way to navigate Reykjavík is the one that suits your style and budget. So, whether you're a budget traveler on foot, a cycling enthusiast, or a car rental adventurer, embrace the city's rhythm, explore its hidden alleys, and discover the magic that awaits around every corner.

Did You Know: Reykjavík isn't afraid to embrace its fiery origins. Public buildings and homes are often heated by geothermal energy sourced from the smoldering heart of the island. Take a dip in the Blue Lagoon or visit the Landmannalaugar Geothermal Pool for a taste of volcanic warmth.

Unpacking Reykjavík: Experiences Beyond the Guidebooks

Reykjavík, Iceland's captivating capital, pulsates with a rhythm beyond just stunning landmarks and geothermal baths. This city is a cultural kaleidoscope, where Viking sagas intertwine with avant-garde art, and ancient traditions weave through vibrant festivals. So, ditch the generic sightseeing checklists and dive into these unforgettable Reykjavík experiences:

The Cultural Tapestry
- **Museum Hopping:** Iceland's history echoes within its museums. Explore the National Museum and delve into Viking settlements, marvel at ancient relics at the Reykjavík City Museum, or lose yourself in the immersive narratives of the Saga Museum. For contemporary art, visit the Reykjavík Art Museum, with its rotating exhibitions, or discover hidden gems like the Kjarvalsstaðir collection housed in a stunning former residence.

- **Gallery Prowls:** The streets of Reykjavík are canvases for artistic expression. Wander through Laugavegur and stumble upon independent galleries showcasing Icelandic talent. Explore hidden alleys in the Grandi district, where murals transform buildings into open-air museums. Don't miss the bustling Kolaportið flea market, where hidden treasures mingle with local creations.
- **Theater Magic:** Immerse yourself in the drama unfolding on Icelandic stages. The National Theatre of Iceland delivers powerful performances, while smaller venues like Tjarnarbíó offer experimental works and avant-garde productions. Catch a comedy show at Laugavegur 110, or be captivated by the National Ballet's graceful movements.
- **Music in the Midnight Sun:** Let the sounds of Iceland wash over you. Catch a classical concert at Harpa, where acoustics and architecture sing in harmony. Listen to contemporary Icelandic bands at cozy cafes or uncover the underground music scene at intimate venues like Gaukurinn. If you're lucky enough to visit during the summer solstice, experience the magic of midnight concerts under the never-setting sun.

Seasonal Celebrations

Iceland's cultural calendar bursts with vibrant festivals, weaving tradition and modern flair. If your visit coincides with one of these, consider yourself lucky:

- **Winter Lights Festival:** In February, Reykjavík transforms into a wonderland of light installations, illuminating the city with artistic brilliance. Immerse yourself in interactive displays, witness dazzling projections, and partake in workshops and concerts that celebrate the transformative power of light during the darkest days.
- **Secret Lagoon Festival:** During the first weekend of August, the iconic Secret Lagoon comes alive with music, food, and local artisans. Soak in the geothermal waters, sample Icelandic delicacies, and dance under the midnight sun. It's a truly unique Icelandic experience.
- **Culture Night:** In August, Reykjavík's museums, galleries, and cultural institutions stay open late, offering free performances, exhibitions, and activities. Embrace the city's infectious energy as

art spills onto the streets and music fills the air.

Themed Tours

Beyond the usual sightseeing tours, Reykjavík offers unique experiences to tap into specific interests:

- **Foodie Tours:** Sample Iceland's culinary delights on a food tour, from fresh seafood and lamb dishes to artisanal cheeses and fermented shark (if you dare!). Explore local markets, hidden restaurants, and traditional food shops, discovering the soul of Iceland on your plate.
- **Ghost Walk Tours**: Investigate Reykjavík's darker side with a ghost walk tour. Navigate narrow alleys and hear chilling tales of hauntings, folklore, and historical mysteries that will send shivers down your spine.
- **Northern Lights Chasing:** If your Icelandic adventure falls during the fall or winter months, join a Northern Lights tour. Venture beyond the city lights and gaze up at the sky, mesmerized by the emerald, crimson, and violet hues dancing across the canvas of the night.

Reykjavík is more than just a checklist of sights. It's a city to be felt, savored, and experienced. So, open your heart, embrace the cultural tapestry, and weave your Icelandic odyssey, one unforgettable experience at a time.

Did You Know: During the summer solstice, Reykjavík basks in the glow of the midnight sun. There's no need to set an alarm. Explore the city under the unending daylight, catch a late-night concert, or indulge in a sunrise picnic on Mount Esja.

Run Wild with Family Adventures

Reykjavík might conjure images of volcanic landscapes and geothermal wonders, but it's also a treasure trove of family-friendly activities that will have your little ones bouncing with excitement. From playful penguins and majestic whales to steaming hot springs and otherworldly glaciers, Reykjavík promises an unforgettable adventure for all ages.

Sparkling City Fun

- **Reykjavík Zoo:** Journey through the animal kingdom at the Reykjavík Zoo, a haven for Arctic foxes, playful seals, and even reindeer. Let the kids marvel at the snow leopards, giggle at the mischievous monkeys, and learn about the importance of conservation in this cozy zoo nestled within the city.

- **Whaley Good Time:** Embark on a whale-watching adventure and witness the giants of the ocean in their natural habitat. Sail out from Reykjavík harbor and watch in awe as humpback whales breach, dolphins frolic, and playful minke whales slice through the water. The sheer size and grace of these creatures will leave a lasting impression on the whole family.
- **Splash and Play:** Let loose at Laugardalur Park, a sprawling oasis of green in the middle of the city. Children will love the playground equipment, water features, and miniature golf course. Pack a picnic basket, rent a paddle boat on the lake, or simply relax in the sunshine and soak up the joyful atmosphere.
- **Museum Magic:** Dive into the interactive exhibits at the Reykjavík Maritime Museum, where children can climb aboard historic ships, learn about Iceland's seafaring history, and even try their hand at sailing simulations. For a dose of science and wonder, visit Perlan, where glaciers come alive through multimedia displays and the Northern Lights dance across the ceiling.

Beyond the City Walls

- **Golden Circle Wonders:** Step into a wonderland of fire and ice with a day trip to the Golden Circle. Explore the cascading Gullfoss waterfall, feel the earth tremble at the Geysir geothermal area, and descend into the volcanic crater of Kerið. Pack your swimsuits and take a dip in the Secret Lagoon, a natural geothermal pool nestled amidst lava fields, for a truly magical experience.
- **Snæfellsnes Peninsula:** Nicknamed "Iceland in Miniature," the Snæfellsnes Peninsula offers a taste of everything the country has to offer. Hike on glaciers, explore black sand beaches, marvel at basalt columns, and even spot seals basking on the rocks. Kids will love the Snæfellsjökull glacier, the backdrop of Jules Verne's "Journey to the Center of the Earth," and the Arnarstapi sea stacks, home to countless nesting birds.
- **Jökulsárlón Glacier Lagoon:** Witness the awe-inspiring beauty of Jökulsárlón Glacier Lagoon, a glistening turquoise lake dotted with icebergs like diamonds scattered on the water. Take a boat

tour amongst the ice giants, listen to the cracking and calving sounds, and capture breathtaking photos of this otherworldly landscape.
- **Reykjadalur Hot Spring Thermal River:** For a truly unique experience, head to Reykjadalur Valley, where a geothermal river winds its way through the mountains. Let the children dig hot spring pools in the soft sand, relax in the warm water, and soak up the stunning scenery of snow-capped peaks and moss-covered valleys.

Tips for a Smooth Family Adventure:
- Pack for all weather conditions, including layers, waterproof gear, and sturdy shoes.
- Pre-book tours and activities during peak season to avoid disappointment.
- Consider purchasing the Reykjavík City Card for discounted entry to museums and public transportation.
- Embrace the Icelandic pace and schedule breaks for snacks and playtime.
- Most importantly, let loose, have fun, and create memories that will last a lifetime.

Reykjavík is a playground for families, a gateway to natural wonders, and a canvas for unforgettable experiences. So, pack your sense of adventure, grab your little explorers, and get ready to discover the magic of Reykjavík, one family adventure at a time.

Did You Know: Reykjavík boasts a vibrant art scene, from street murals that splash color across buildings to quirky independent galleries exhibiting contemporary Icelandic works. Be surprised by the unexpected artistic gems tucked away in hidden corners of the city.

Reykjavík's Culinary Canvas: A Feast for the Senses

Reykjavík is a city where hot springs bubble and geysers erupt, but the real heat is found in its culinary scene. From melt-in-your-mouth seafood to hearty lamb dishes and surprising fermented delicacies, Reykjavík's restaurants and markets offer a taste of Iceland's unique culinary heritage that will tantalize your taste buds and paint a vibrant picture of the country's culture.

Dive into the Ocean's Bounty

- **Fish Market:** Start your culinary adventure at the Reykjavík Fish Market, a bustling hub of fresh seafood. Sample succulent langoustines, savor melt-in-your-mouth cod cheeks, and marvel at the array of glistening fish straight from the icy North Atlantic. Grab a bite at one of the stalls, or take your catch home for a DIY seafood feast.

- **Fish and Chips by the Harbor:** No trip to Reykjavík is complete without indulging in classic fish and chips. Grab a paper-wrapped parcel and head to the harbor, where the salty breeze and seagull cries provide the perfect soundtrack to your meal. Bite into crispy batter, savor the tender fish, and let the ocean spray awaken your senses.

A Taste of Icelandic Tradition

- **Bæjarins Beztu Pylsur:** No culinary tour of Reykjavík is complete without a visit to Bæjarins Beztu Pylsur, the world-famous hot dog stand. These small, lamb-based hot dogs, topped with crispy onions and mustard, are a national icon and a must-try for any food enthusiast.

- **Lamb-Tastic Delights:** Iceland is lamb country, and you won't want to miss out on its succulent flavors. Try the traditional "hangikjöt," a slow-smoked lamb, at Þrír Frakkar. For a modern twist, head to Dill, where lamb becomes a canvas for creative culinary artistry.

- **Adventurous Bites:** For the adventurous palate, Iceland offers unique delicacies like "hákarl," fermented shark. Sample this pungent treat at a local market or restaurant, and brace yourself for a truly memorable (and possibly eye-watering) experience.

Market Marvels

- **Hlemmur Food Hall:** Immerse yourself in the vibrant atmosphere of Hlemmur Food Hall, a culinary melting pot housed in a former bus terminal. From traditional Icelandic fare to Asian noodles and Latin American flavors, there's something for every taste bud under one roof. Grab a bite from different stalls, chat with local vendors, and experience the city's culinary pulse.

- **Kolaportið Flea Market:** This treasure trove of vintage finds also hides a delicious secret. Tucked away amongst the clothing and antiques are stalls brimming with Icelandic delicacies. Sample smoked salmon, homemade jams, and traditional pastries, and discover a taste of Icelandic culture with every bite.

Beyond the City Walls

- **Farm-to-Table Feast:** For a truly authentic experience, venture outside the city and visit a working farm. Enjoy a farm-to-table meal, where fresh ingredients are plucked straight from the land and transformed into hearty, home-cooked dishes. Learn about traditional farming practices, meet the friendly animals, and savor the taste of Iceland's rural charm.

Sweet Endings

No meal is complete without a sweet treat. Indulge in Icelandic skyr, a thick and creamy yogurt topped with fresh berries and homemade granola. For a taste of local tradition, try "kleina," deep-fried twisted pastries dusted with sugar, a perfect treat to accompany a hot cup of coffee.

Tips for a Delicious Adventure:

- Reservations are recommended at popular restaurants, especially during peak season.
- Don't be afraid to try new things. Icelandic cuisine offers a unique and exciting culinary adventure.
- Tap water is safe to drink in Reykjavík, so ditch the bottled water and stay hydrated.
- Be mindful of tipping. In Iceland, tipping is not expected but always appreciated.

Reykjavík's culinary scene is a window into the country's culture, traditions, and vibrant spirit. So, grab your appetite, wander through bustling markets, explore cozy restaurants, and savor the unique flavors that Iceland has to offer. Your taste buds will thank you, and your memories will be forever enriched by the culinary canvas of Reykjavík.

Shopping in Reykjavík: From Laugavegur's Buzz to Hidden Gems

Beneath the midnight sun and Northern Lights in Reykjavík, a captivating shopping scene thrives, offering everything from quirky souvenirs to high-end fashion. Whether you're a seasoned thrift hunter or a luxury-label aficionado, Reykjavík has something to tempt your wallet and fill your bags with unique treasures.

Strolling Down Laugavegur

No shopping spree in Reykjavík is complete without a saunter down Laugavegur, the city's beating heart. Lined with colorful buildings and buzzing with energy, this main artery offers a delightful array of shops. Browse trendy Icelandic design at Kron by Kron, where sleek sweaters and playful accessories await. Pop into Skólabrú for whimsical homewares and gifts. Then, fuel your shopping spree with a pastry at Sandholt Bakari, where the aroma of freshly baked bread is an irresistible siren call.

Beyond the Main Drag

Venture beyond Laugavegur and discover hidden gems on side streets like Skólavörðustígur. Find vintage treasures at Vintage 101, where clothing racks whisper tales of past adventures. Indulge your inner bibliophile at Mál og Menning bookstore, a haven for Icelandic literature and charming trinkets. For contemporary art and stunning jewelry, wander into Iðunn, a gallery-meets-shop exhibiting the talents of local artists.

Mall Marvels

For a dose of modern convenience, step into Kringlan Shopping Mall, a glass-and-steel oasis housing over 100 stores. Browse international brands such as Hugo Boss and Lacoste, pick up souvenirs at Kiosk, or simply indulge in some retail therapy during a rainy afternoon. Kringlan also boasts a cinema, restaurants, and even a supermarket, making it a one-stop shop for all your needs.

Market Finds and Treasure Troves

For a delightful dose of Icelandic quirkiness, head to Kolaportið Flea Market, a cacophony of smells and sounds where you can unearth vintage clothing, handmade crafts, Viking-inspired memorabilia, and even fermented shark. Haggling is encouraged, so brush up your bargaining skills and dive into this treasure trove of unexpected finds.

For a curated selection of local handicrafts and art, explore Reykjavík Flea Market. Held regularly at various locations, these markets present a unique opportunity to meet local artisans, admire their creations, and take home a piece of Icelandic magic. From hand-knitted sweaters to intricate jewelry and quirky souvenirs, you'll find something special to remember your Icelandic adventure.

Tips for Savvy Shoppers:
- **Go Cashless:** Visa and Mastercard are widely accepted, but carrying some Icelandic krona is always handy for smaller purchases.
- **Consider the VAT Refund:** Tourists can claim a VAT refund on purchases exceeding 4,999 ISK.
- **Shop Early:** Popular items and limited-edition pieces tend to sell out quickly, so visit stores earlier in the day.
- **Respect Local Traditions:** Haggling is acceptable at flea markets, but be polite and fair in your negotiations.

Reykjavík's shopping scene is a tapestry woven with trendy boutiques, hidden gems, and vibrant markets. So, ditch the generic souvenirs and explore the city's retail labyrinth. From Laugavegur's bustling energy to Kolaportið's quirky charm, each shop, market, and mall whispers a unique story. Unpack your shopping bags, let your curiosity guide you, and discover the treasures that await in Reykjavík's retail wonderland.

A Guide to Reykjavík Accommodation

Reykjavík beckons with its geothermal wonders, midnight sun, and vibrant cultural scene. On your Icelandic odyssey, finding the perfect accommodation sets the stage for your experience. Whether you're a budget-conscious backpacker, a luxury seeker, or a family looking for a home away from home, Reykjavík offers a diverse range of options to suit every need and budget.

Budget-Friendly Beds:
- **Hostels:** For social butterflies and solo travelers, Reykjavík's hostels offer a chance to connect with fellow adventurers. KEX Hostel, housed in a former biscuit factory, boasts a trendy atmosphere and cozy pods, while Loft Hostel provides stylish shared rooms and a vibrant common area. Hostels often organize events and tours, making them a great base for exploring the city

and making new friends.
- **Guesthouses and Apartments**: For a little more privacy and comfort without breaking the bank, consider a guesthouse or apartment. These cozy accommodations offer independent living spaces and kitchens, allowing you to cook your meals and save on restaurant costs. Check out Guesthouse Sunna for its charming atmosphere and central location or Fosshotel Baron for its modern amenities and quirky décor.

Mid-Range Magic:
- **Boutique Hotels**: For those seeking a touch of luxury without exorbitant prices, Reykjavík's boutique hotels offer a charming escape. Hotel Fron, with its minimalist design and rooftop terrace views, is a popular choice.

Luxury Lodgings:
- **High-End Hotels**: For those who appreciate the finer things, Reykjavík's luxury hotels offer unparalleled comfort and service. The Reykjavík EDITION, with its sleek design and panoramic city views, is a haven of sophistication. For a touch of history and grandeur, consider Hotel Borg, housed in a former bank building and boasting a Michelin-starred restaurant.
- **Private Villas and Retreats**: For the ultimate indulgence, consider renting a private villa or retreat. These luxurious havens offer privacy, stunning views, and personalized services like private chefs and in-house activities. Imagine relaxing in your geothermal hot tub while gazing at the Northern Lights. This is pure Icelandic bliss.

Beyond the Walls:
- **Airbnb and Guesthouses**: For a local experience, consider staying outside of the city center in an Airbnb or guesthouse. You'll get a taste of Icelandic life, enjoy lower prices, and have a chance to interact with locals. Explore charming towns like Akureyri or Vík í Mýrdal for a truly authentic Icelandic experience.

Making the Choice:
- **Consider Your Budget**: Reykjavík's accommodation options cater to all budgets. Prioritize your needs and compare prices before booking.

- **Location Is Key:** Choose a location that suits your needs. Do you want to be in the heart of the action or enjoy a quieter setting?
- **Travel Style Matters:** Are you a solo traveler seeking adventure or a family looking for comfort? Choose accommodation that matches your travel style.
- **Think about Amenities:** Consider what amenities are important to you, such as breakfast, Wi-Fi, or on-site parking.

Remember:
- Book early, especially during peak season, to secure the best deals and availability.
- Many accommodations offer special packages and deals, so do your research.
- Ask for recommendations from locals or travel experts.

Finding the perfect accommodation in Reykjavík is part of the adventure. Embrace the Icelandic spirit, explore your options, and find your dream home base for your unforgettable journey to the Land of Fire and Ice.

Hidden Gems and Practical Tips for a Magical Adventure

Beyond Reykjavík's iconic landmarks and midnight sun lies a treasure trove of hidden gems and practical tips that will elevate your Icelandic adventure to new heights. So, ditch the guidebooks and delve into these secrets.

Nature Unleashed:
- **Secret Lagoon Soak:** Skip the Blue Lagoon crowds and head to the Secret Lagoon, nestled in lava fields. Bathe in geothermal bliss under the open sky, savoring the natural beauty and fewer faces.
- **Elliðaár Art Trail:** Hike the scenic Elliðaár trail, weaving through geothermal vents, waterfalls, and moss-covered valleys. Along the way, discover sculptures hidden in the wild terrain, adding an artistic twist to your nature walk.

Cultural Gems:
- **Reykjavík City Library:** Escape the tourist trail and find tranquility in the stunning Reykjavík City Library. Browse

Icelandic literature, soak in the panoramic views, and savor the serene atmosphere.
- **Secret Cinema:** Catch a movie at Bíó Paradís, Reykjavík's hidden gem cinema. This art deco theater screens independent films and classics, often with delicious cocktails and cozy vibes.

Foodie Delights:
- **Fish and Chips with a View:** Ditch the crowded harbors and head to Akureyri, a tiny fishing village just outside Reykjavík. Grab freshly caught fish and chips and settle on the pebbled beach for an unforgettable feast while you enjoy the ocean views.
- **Brynjunn the Baker:** Skip the generic bakeries and indulge in the sourdough heaven at Brynjunn the Baker. Sample traditional "kleinur" pastries and melt-in-your-mouth rye bread baked with generations-old techniques.

Practical Pointers:
- **Embrace the City Card:** Purchase the Reykjavík City Card for free public transportation, museum entry discounts, and thermal pool access – a savvy traveler's best friend.
- **Download Useful Apps:** Get ahead of the game with apps like Citymapper for navigation, Strætó for bus schedules, and Mynbar to find happy hour deals.
- **Cash Is King (Sometimes):** While Visa and Mastercard are widely accepted, carry some Icelandic krona for smaller purchases and street vendors.
- **Warm Layers are Key:** Be prepared for unpredictable weather. Pack layers, waterproof gear, and sturdy shoes for spontaneous adventures.

Reykjavík whispers its secrets to those who listen closely. So, wander off the beaten path, embrace local gems, and let these practical tips be your compass. Unravel the hidden layers of this vibrant city and discover the magic that awaits beyond the surface. Happy Reykjavík adventures!

Chapter 4: Reykjanes Peninsula, the Golden Circle and the South Coast

Iceland's volcanic heart beats loud on the Reykjanes Peninsula, where smoldering lava fields whisper tales of fiery creation. But venture south, and the ocean takes center stage, roaring across black sand beaches and carving dramatic cliffs into the coastline. Prepare to be embraced by fire and serenaded by the ocean's symphony as you delve into this captivating corner of Iceland, section by section.

First, you ignite your journey on the Reykjanes Peninsula, a land born from molten fury. From bubbling mud pools and geothermal wonders like the Blue Lagoon to volcanic landscapes and charming fishing villages, this fiery peninsula promises an adventure like no other.

Next, you'll trace the Golden Circle, Iceland's classic tourist route, where waterfalls roar, geysers erupt, and tectonic plates dance. Prepare to marvel at Gullfoss's thunderous cascade, feel the earth tremble at Geysir, and descend into the volcanic crater of Kerið.

Finally, you'll navigate the dramatic tapestry of the South Coast, where glaciers whisper secrets to the sea, and black sand beaches stretch beneath endless skies. Witness the ethereal beauty of Jökulsárlón glacier lagoon, explore the charming village of Vík í Mýrdal, and stand in awe before the powerful Skógafoss waterfall.

So, buckle up, dear reader, for this chapter promises an expedition through fire and ice, where molten dreams sculpt landscapes and ocean symphonies fill the air. It's time to unravel the secrets of the Reykjanes Peninsula and the South Coast, one stunning vista at a time.

The Reykjanes Peninsula's location.
A Red Cherry, CC BY-SA 4.0 <https://creativecommons.org/licenses/by-sa/4.0>, via Wikimedia Commons. https://commons.wikimedia.org/wiki/File:Reykjanes_Sudurnes.png

Reykjanes Peninsula: Iceland's Fiery Gateway with Geothermal Delights

The Reykjanes Peninsula, jutting out like a fiery fist from Iceland's mainland, is more than just the landing point for most visitors. This volcanic playground, home to Keflavík International Airport, packs a punch with its rugged landscapes, bubbling geothermal wonders, and a fascinating history rooted in fire and ice.

Historical Background:

Reykjanes Peninsula played a pivotal role in Iceland's settlement. Vikings first landed here in 874 AD, drawn by the fertile coastal plains and abundant geothermal resources. The peninsula is also home to the Þingvellir National Park, where the Icelandic parliament first convened in 930 AD, marking the birthplace of democracy in Iceland.

Reykjanes Peninsula.
Vincent van Zeijst, CC BY 3.0 <https://creativecommons.org/licenses/by/3.0>, via Wikimedia Commons. https://commons.wikimedia.org/wiki/File:Iceland_(3),_Reykjanes_peninsula.JPG

Main Attractions:

- **Blue Lagoon:** Iceland's crown jewel, this milky blue geothermal oasis nestled in lava fields offers a luxurious soak in naturally heated waters rich in minerals. Relax in the steam and soak up the stunning views of the surrounding landscape.

As of the writing of this book, the standard operating hours are from 8 AM to 10 PM. Please double-check the opening hours online should there have been any slight change in their schedule.

Blue Lagoon.
JavierOlivares, CC BY-SA 4.0 <https://creativecommons.org/licenses/by-sa/4.0>, via Wikimedia Commons: https://commons.wikimedia.org/wiki/File:The_Blue_Lagoon_2.jpg

- **Kleifarvatn Lake:** Iceland's largest lake by volume, surrounded by stunning scenery and offering hiking trails and geothermal springs on its shores. Take a boat tour on the lake's glassy surface, hike through the surrounding volcanic terrain, or soak in the warm waters of geothermal pools hidden on the lake's perimeter.

  As of the writing of this book, you can visit Kleifarvatn Lake at any time of the day and any day of the week.

Kleifarvatn Lake.
Joe deSousa, CC0, via Wikimedia Commons:
https://commons.wikimedia.org/wiki/File:Lake_Kleifarvatn,_Iceland_(41495264840).jpg

- **Gunnuhver Hot Springs:** Witness the raw power of Mother Earth at these bubbling mud pools and fumaroles, spewing steam and emitting sulfuric scents. Feel the ground tremble beneath your feet and marvel at the vibrant colors and textures created by geothermal activity.

As of the writing of this book, Gunnuhver Hot Springs are open 24 hours a day, every day.

Gunnuhver Hot Springs.
Christian Bickel, CC BY-SA 2.0 DE <https://creativecommons.org/licenses/by-sa/2.0/de/deed.en>, via Wikimedia Commons: https://commons.wikimedia.org/wiki/File:Gunnuhver_4.jpg

- **Reykjanesviti Lighthouse:** Perched on the southern tip of the peninsula, this historic lighthouse offers panoramic views of the rugged coastline and crashing waves. Climb the spiral staircase to the top and imagine the lives of lighthouse keepers who once braved the elements here.

As of the writing of this book, the normal opening hours are 24 hours a day, seven days a week.

Reykjanesviti Lighthouse.
Wolfgang Fricke, CC BY 3.0 <https://creativecommons.org/licenses/by/3.0>, via Wikimedia Commons: https://commons.wikimedia.org/wiki/File:Reykjanesviti_Lighthouse,_Iceland.jpg

- **Valahnúkamöl Cliffs:** Dramatic black sand cliffs sculpted by the ocean winds, home to nesting seabirds and offering breathtaking coastal scenery. Hike along the cliff tops, feel the spray of the ocean on your face, and witness the power of the North Atlantic as it crashes against the volcanic rock.

As of the writing of this book, the normal opening hours 24 hours a day, seven days a week.

Valahnúkamöl cliffs.
Joe deSousa, CC0, via Wikimedia Commons:
https://commons.wikimedia.org/wiki/File:Valahn%C3%BAkam%C3%B6l,_Iceland_(44288091430).jpg

Transport:
- **Car Rental:** The best way to explore the peninsula's diverse attractions at your own pace. Reykjavik Car Rental or Blue Car Rental offer reliable options with convenient pick-up at Keflavík airport.
- **Public Bus:** Strætó buses connect Keflavík to various points on the peninsula, making it a budget-friendly option for those without a car.
- **Day Tours:** Numerous tour operators offer organized trips from Reykjavik, covering some of the top highlights. This is a great option for those who want a guided experience and don't have much time.

Did You Know: Reykjanes is one of the most seismically active areas in Iceland, home to over 200 volcanoes, some dormant and others simmering beneath the surface. The earth here is young, barely 6 million years old, making it a geologist's paradise.

Experiences:
- **Whale Watching:** Embark on a boat tour from Grindavík or Reykjavík to witness the majestic humpback whales, dolphins,

and porpoises frolicking in the North Atlantic. Keep an eye out for other marine life, like puffins and seals, as you navigate the icy waters.
- **Horseback Riding:** Experience the wild beauty of the landscape on horseback, with tours available for all levels through companies like Íshestar Farm and Eldhestar Horseback Riding. Gallop across black sand beaches, traverse geothermal fields, and feel the wind in your hair as you connect with these iconic Icelandic animals.
- **Northern Lights Chasing:** During winter months, when the nights grow long, and the sky is alive with dancing lights of emerald and turquoise, join a guided tour in search of the mesmerizing aurora borealis. Drive away from light pollution, wait patiently under the starry expanse, and be awestruck by the celestial light show, a truly magical experience.
- **Culinary Adventures:** Embark on a food tour to discover the unique flavors of the Reykjanes Peninsula. Sample fresh seafood caught locally, indulge in homemade lamb dishes, and try traditional Icelandic treats like "kleinur" pastries and "skyr" yogurt. Learn about the culinary traditions and meet the passionate producers behind the region's delicious offerings.

Did You Know: The Reykjanes peninsula is situated on the Mid-Atlantic Ridge, where the Eurasian and North American tectonic plates are slowly pulling apart. You can walk between the continents at the Bridge Between Continents in Sandvik, a surreal experience where moss carpets straddle the crack between worlds.

Family Fun:
- **Viking World:** Journey back in time at this interactive museum dedicated to the Viking era. Children can try on replica armor, participate in traditional games, and learn about Viking culture through exhibits and storytelling.

Did You Know: Local legend tells of a mischievous troll named Grýla, who resides in the mountains of Reykjanes. Her thirteen terrifying sons, the Yule Lads, visit Icelandic children during the 13 nights leading up to Christmas, leaving small gifts or mischievous pranks depending on their behavior.

Where to Eat:

- **Lava Restaurant:** Nestled in the geothermal landscape of Svartabrunn, Lava Restaurant offers a unique dining experience with panoramic views and creative dishes inspired by volcanic heat. Sample the smoked lamb or the geothermal-baked bread for a taste of the peninsula's fiery spirit.

- **Take Off Bistro:** Recharge after a day of exploring at this charming bistro. Grab a steaming cup of coffee, indulge in homemade pastries, and enjoy the cozy atmosphere before your next adventure.

- **Brynjarfoss Restaurant:** Located near Skálholt, this cozy restaurant overlooking the Brúnafoss waterfall offers a delightful menu featuring fresh local ingredients and scenic views. Sample the grilled langoustine, the lamb shoulder, or the vegetarian options, all paired with local wines or beers.

Shopping Guide:

- **Saltfiskstofa Íslands:** Discover the traditional Icelandic delicacy of fermented shark at this specialty store in Grindavík. Learn about the unique production process, sample different flavors, and even purchase a piece (if you dare!) to take home as a souvenir.

- **Handverk Duus:** Find handcrafted Icelandic souvenirs and treasures at this shop in Keflavík. Browse through wool sweaters, jewelry made with volcanic rock, and other unique pieces crafted by local artisans.

- **Viking World Gift Shop:** Stock up on Viking-themed souvenirs at the gift shop within the Viking World museum. Find replicas of helmets and weapons, books on Norse mythology, and clothing inspired by the Viking era, perfect for history buffs and souvenir hunters.

Accommodations:

- **Kleifarvatn Cottages:** Immerse yourself in nature at Kleifarvatn Cottages, nestled on the shores of the lake. Choose from cozy cabins or traditional turf houses and enjoy the peaceful surroundings with easy access to hiking trails and geothermal springs.

- **Hotel Keflavik:** Located conveniently near Keflavík airport, this modern hotel offers comfortable rooms, delicious dining options, and a relaxed atmosphere for those looking for a convenient base.

Entertainment:
- **Viking Festival:** Immerse yourself in Viking culture during the annual Viking Festival held in June in Hafnafjörður. Witness re-enactments of battles, participate in traditional games, and enjoy live music and performances.
- **Secret Lagoon:** Escape the crowds of the Blue Lagoon and experience a more authentic geothermal soak at the Secret Lagoon. Nestled in lava fields, this natural pool offers a serene atmosphere and a chance to connect with fellow travelers.
- **Live music nights:** Many bars and restaurants in Keflavík and Grindavík host live music nights featuring local musicians and bands. Enjoy a drink, listen to Icelandic tunes, and soak up the vibrant atmosphere.
- **Stargazing:** Iceland's remote location and low light pollution make it a paradise for stargazing. Find a dark spot away from light pollution, lie back on the ground, and marvel at the breathtaking view of the Milky Way and constellations.

Sports and Leisure:
- **Hiking and Biking:** Explore the varied landscapes of the Reykjanes Peninsula on foot or by bike. Hike through lava fields, climb volcanic craters, and cycle along scenic coastal paths.
- **Sailing and Kayaking:** Explore the coastline from a different perspective by taking a sailing or kayaking tour. Witness hidden coves, spot marine life, and enjoy the feeling of gliding through the ocean waters.
- **Surfing:** Iceland's rugged coastline offers some of the best surfing waves in Europe for experienced surfers. Brave the cold waters and test your skills in spots like Hellissandur and Stokksnes.

Hot Spring Etiquette

Iceland's geothermal pools offer a blissful way to melt away stress and soak in the country's natural wonders. But before you dive in, remember that hot springs are shared spaces with their cultural norms. To ensure a harmonious experience for everyone, follow these simple guidelines:
- **Shower before You Soak:** This isn't a suggestion; it's a requirement. Rinse off thoroughly with soap and shampoo

before entering any pool, public or private. It's not just about hygiene; it shows respect for your fellow bathers.
- **Leave on Your Swimsuit:** While some European countries embrace nudity in geothermal pools, Iceland is more conservative. Wearing a swimsuit is mandatory in most public pools and even in private geothermally heated hot tubs. Respecting local customs is appreciated.
- **Don't Jump or Splash:** These pools are often small and shared, so be mindful of others. Avoid boisterous behavior, jumping in, or splashing excessively. Relax, unwind, and let the tranquility of the warm water envelop you.
- **Mind Your Towel:** Keep your towel on dry ground outside the pool area. Drape it neatly on a designated rack, not on benches or the poolside, to prevent moisture and slipping hazards.
- **Respect the Locals:** Remember, hot springs are an important part of Icelandic culture. Be respectful of residents enjoying their leisure time, avoid talking loudly, and maintain a peaceful atmosphere.

With its captivating landscapes, geothermal wonders, and rich history, the Reykjanes Peninsula offers an unforgettable experience for travelers of all kinds. Whether you're seeking adventure, relaxation, or cultural immersion, this fiery gateway to Iceland has something to ignite your spirit. Pack your bags, embrace the geothermal energy, and get ready to explore the wonders of the Reykjanes Peninsula!

The Golden Circle: Iceland's Golden Trek of Wonders

Iceland's Golden Circle, a shimmering loop roughly 300 kilometers in length, pulsates with natural wonders and whispers tales of Viking sagas and ancient geological forces. This classic tourist route packs a punch, showing Iceland's raw beauty in three iconic stops, including Þingvellir National Park, the Geysir geothermal area, and Gullfoss Waterfall. But venture beyond the headline acts; the Golden Circle unravels a tapestry of hidden gems, charming towns, and geothermal marvels waiting to be explored.

Historical Background:

Þingvellir National Park holds a special place in Icelandic history. The world's first recorded parliament convened here in 930 AD, marking the genesis of Iceland's democratic spirit. Tectonic plates shift beneath the surface, carving dramatic landscapes and leaving behind the Almannagjá Gorge, where Vikings held their historic gatherings.

Main Attractions:

- **Þingvellir National Park**: Dive between continents at the Silfra fissure, a crystal-clear rift where North American and Eurasian tectonic plates diverge. Hike scenic trails through lava fields and moss-covered rocks and glimpse Þingvallavatn, Iceland's largest natural lake.

As of the writing of this book, the normal opening hours are 24 hours a day, every day, but the vistor center is only open from 9 AM to 5 PM. Please double-check the opening hours online should there have been any slight change in their schedule.

Þingvellir National Park.
Jakub Hałun, CC BY-SA 4.0 <https://creativecommons.org/licenses/by-sa/4.0>, via Wikimedia Commons:
https://commons.wikimedia.org/wiki/File:%C3%9Eingvellir_National_Park,_Iceland,_20230502_1019_4151.jpg

- **Geysir Geothermal Area:** Witness the fiery earth erupt at Strokkur geyser, spouting boiling water skyward every 5-10 minutes. Explore bubbling mud pools, colorful fumaroles, and steaming vents that paint the landscape with a surreal palette.

As of the writing of this book, the site is open 24 hours a day, every day of the week.

- **Gullfoss Waterfall:** Feel the earth tremble and the spray on your face as the mighty Gullfoss thunders down two tiers into a canyon. Walk behind the falls for a unique perspective, marvel at the rainbows arcing through the mist, and soak in the raw power of nature.

As of the writing of this book, the site is open 24 hours a day, every day of the week.

Gullfoss Waterfall.
Jakub Hałun, CC BY-SA 4.0 <https://creativecommons.org/licenses/by-sa/4.0>, via Wikimedia Commons: https://commons.wikimedia.org/wiki/File:Gullfoss,_Iceland,_20230501_1002_3834.jpg

- **Kerid Crater:** Descend into this volcanic crater, a kaleidoscope in tones of rust-red contrasting with the emerald green lake at its bottom. Hike the rim, capture stunning photos, and imagine the fiery eruption that birthed this geological wonder.

  As of the writing of this book, the normal opening hours are from 8:30 AM to 9 PM from June to August, and from September to May, you can visit while there is daylight. Please double-check the opening hours online should there have been any slight change in their schedule.

  Kerid Crater.
  Netha Hussain, CC0, via Wikimedia Commons:
  https://commons.wikimedia.org/wiki/File:Kerid_Crater_04.jpg

- **Hveragerði:** Discover the "flower town" of Hveragerði, where geothermal energy heats greenhouses, allowing flowers to bloom in Iceland's frigid climes. Stroll through vibrant gardens, soak in geothermal pools, and savor a delicious meal fueled by volcanic heat.

- **Skálholt Cathedral:** Explore the ruins of this former bishop's seat and witness remnants of Iceland's religious past. Hike from here to Laugavatn, a geothermal oasis with a natural pool perfect for a soothing soak.

As of the writing of this book, the normal opening hours are from 9 AM to 6 PM every day, but please double-check the opening hours online should there have been any slight change in their schedule.

Skálholt Cathedral.
Cédric Liénart, CC BY-SA 2.0 <https://creativecommons.org/licenses/by-sa/2.0>, via Wikimedia Commons: https://commons.wikimedia.org/wiki/File:Sk%C3%A1lholt_Cathedral_(44485540564).jpg

- **Nesjavellir and Hellisheiðarvirkjun Geothermal Power Plants:** Learn about Iceland's innovative use of geothermal energy at these impressive power plants. Guided tours offer insights into the sustainability efforts and technological advancements driving Iceland's green future.

As of the writing of this book, the normal opening hours are from 9 AM to 6 PM every day, but please double-check the opening hours online should there have been any slight change in their schedule.

Nesjavellir Geothermal Power Plant.
https://commons.wikimedia.org/wiki/File:NesjavellirPowerPlant_edit2.jpg

Did You Know: The Golden Circle's geothermal activity fueled the imagination of early Icelanders, who believed the bubbling springs and spouting geysers were gateways to the underworld.

Transport:
- **Car Rental:** The most convenient way to explore the Golden Circle at your own pace. Many rental agencies offer pick-up and drop-off at Keflavík airport or Reykjavík.
- **Golden Circle Day Tours:** Numerous tour operators offer organized trips from Reykjavík, covering the highlights with guides and transportation. Ideal for those without a car or short

on time.
- **Public Bus:** Strætó buses connect Reykjavík to key Golden Circle stops but are less flexible than other options.

Experiences:
- **Snorkeling in Silfra:** Immerse yourself in the crystal-clear waters of Silfra fissure, marveling at the underwater canyon formed by continental drift. This unique snorkeling or diving experience offers a window into Iceland's geological wonders.
- **Helicopter Tour:** Soar above the Golden Circle, witnessing its spectacular landscapes from a bird's-eye view. This adrenaline-pumping adventure offers breathtaking panoramas of Þingvellir, Geysir, and Gullfoss.
- **Horseback Riding:** Explore the Golden Circle on horseback, traversing fields, riding along geothermal springs, and experiencing the landscape in a traditional Icelandic way. Several companies offer tours for all levels.
- **Northern Lights Chasing:** During the winter months, when emerald and turquoise lights dance across the night sky, embark on a guided tour in search of the mesmerizing aurora borealis. Escape light pollution, wait patiently under the starry expanse, and be awestruck by the celestial show.
- **Lava Tunnel Caving:** Venture into the earth at Víðgelmir lava cave, one of the largest in Iceland. Guided tours take you through tunnels carved by ancient lava flows, revealing fascinating volcanic formations and a glimpse into the island's fiery past.
- **Golden Circle Food Tour:** Discover the region's culinary delights with a guided food tour. Sample fresh produce grown in Hveragerði's geothermal greenhouses, indulge in lamb dishes and traditional skyr yogurt, and learn about Icelandic food culture while touring local farms and producers.
- **Viking History Tour:** Delve into the Viking roots of the Golden Circle at Þingvellir National Park. Stand where historic assemblies took place, visit archaeological sites, and learn about the lives and customs of these early settlers through stories and exhibits.
- **Geopower Exploration:** Dive deeper into Iceland's geothermal energy scene with a tour of the Hellisheiði Power Plant.

Understand the science behind harnessing volcanic heat, explore the plant's inner workings, and learn about the role of renewable energy in Iceland's future.

Family Fun:
- **Secret Lagoon:** Escape the crowds of the Blue Lagoon and experience a more affordable and authentic geothermal soak at the Secret Lagoon near Flúðir. Enjoy the warm waters, natural surroundings, and family-friendly atmosphere.
- **Laugarvatn Geothermal Area:** Hike to the Laugarvatn geothermal oasis, nestled between mountains and boasting a natural swimming pool perfect for a family dip. The geothermal heat keeps the water warm even in winter, making it a year-round destination.

Did You Know: Skálholt, once a prominent religious center, was the birthplace of Snorri Sturluson, a 13th-century poet and historian who preserved Norse mythology in the Prose Edda.

Where to Eat:
- **Friðheimar Tomato Farm:** Savor the unique flavors of Iceland's geothermal-heated greenhouses at Friðheimar Tomato Farm near Selfoss. Enjoy a tomato-themed lunch, sample dishes prepared with these fruits, and explore the innovative greenhouses.
- **Efstidalur Guesthouse and Restaurant:** This family-run establishment near Gullfoss offers traditional Icelandic cuisine with a modern twist. Try the lamb stew, the pan-fried fish, or the homemade skyr for a delicious and authentic meal.
- **Café Flúðir:** Take a break at this charming cafe in Flúðir, which offers homemade pastries, soups, and sandwiches. Warm up with a hot coffee, indulge in a cinnamon roll, and enjoy the relaxed atmosphere before continuing your Golden Circle adventures.

Shopping Guide:
- **The Golden Circle Visitor Center:** Find souvenirs, local crafts, and Icelandic goods at the visitor centers located near Þingvellir National Park and Geysir geothermal area. Support local artisans and take home a piece of Iceland's unique spirit.

- **Hveragerði Geothermal Greenhouse Stores:** Pick up fresh flowers, vegetables, and herbs grown in Hveragerði's geothermal greenhouses. These unique souvenirs from the "flower town" are a charming reminder of Iceland's innovative use of natural resources.
- **Skálholt Cathedral Gift Shop:** Discover historical artifacts and reproductions related to Skálholt's religious past at the cathedral's gift shop. Find Icelandic books, Viking-themed trinkets, and locally made crafts.
- **The Icelandic Store**: Located in various outlets across the Golden Circle, The Icelandic Store offers a vast selection of Icelandic souvenirs, from wool sweaters and volcanic rock jewelry to food products and unique Icelandic design items.

Did You Know: The Nesjavellir and Hellisheiðarvirkjun geothermal power plants are among the cleanest and most efficient in the world, harnessing Iceland's natural heat to generate renewable energy.

Accommodations:

- **ION Adventure Hotel:** For a truly unique experience, stay at the ION Adventure Hotel near Selfoss, where futuristic glass pods offer stunning views of the Northern Lights and surrounding landscapes.
- **Hótel Geysir:** Located conveniently near the Geysir geothermal area, Hótel Geysir offers comfortable rooms and delicious dining options with panoramic views of the volcanic landscape.
- **Laugarvatn Cottages:** Immerse yourself in nature at Laugarvatn Cottages, nestled near the geothermal oasis. Choose from cozy cabins or traditional turf houses and enjoy the peaceful surroundings with easy access to hiking trails and hot springs.
- **Skálholt Farm Guesthouse:** Experience Icelandic farm life at Skálholt Farm Guesthouse, offering comfortable rooms and traditional meals prepared with local ingredients. Explore the surrounding countryside, learn about sustainable farming practices, and soak in the historical atmosphere of this former bishopric.

Sports and Leisure:

- **Hiking and Biking:** Explore the diverse landscapes of the Golden Circle on foot or by bike. Hike through lava fields, climb volcanic

craters, and cycle along scenic trails past Gullfoss and Þingvellir. Numerous routes cater to all fitness levels.
- **Fishing:** Cast your line in the rivers and lakes around the Golden Circle, including Hvítá River near Þingvellir, known for its abundance of brown trout and salmon. Fishing licenses are readily available, and guided tours can be arranged for those unfamiliar with the local waters.
- **Golfing:** Tee off at the unique Laugarvatn Golf Course, designed around the geothermal oasis. Enjoy breathtaking views of the mountains and geothermal pools while perfecting your swing on this 18-hole course.
- **Snowmobiling and Glacier Adventures:** During the winter months, embark on a thrilling snowmobile adventure across glaciers near the Golden Circle, experiencing the raw power and beauty of these icy giants. Guided tours offer adrenaline-pumping expeditions for those seeking winter thrills.

With its awe-inspiring landscapes, geothermal wonders, and historical significance, the Golden Circle offers an unforgettable experience for travelers of all ages and interests. Whether you're a history buff, a nature enthusiast, or a seeker of adventure, this route unveils Iceland's magic one breathtaking stop at a time.

The South Coast: Iceland's Symphony of Ice and Fire

Iceland's South Coast, stretching its dramatic spine from Seljalandsfoss to Vík í Mýrdal, is a symphony of glacial whispers and volcanic roars. Here, glaciers carve valleys under skies sculpted by ash plumes, waterfalls thunder into the ocean, and black sand beaches sing ancient tales of fire and ice. Immerse yourself in this wild symphony, where Viking sagas unfold in the stunning landscapes and hidden gems await discovery.

Historical Background:

The South Coast boasts a rich tapestry of history. Vikings first landed here in the 9th century, drawn by fertile plains and abundant fishing grounds. The region witnessed battles, sagas unfolded, and folklore took root in the raw beauty of its landscapes. Eyjafjallajökull's 2010 eruption is a stark reminder of the earth's fiery power, forever etching its mark on the region's memory.

Main Attractions:
- **Jökulsárlón Glacier Lagoon:** Witness the majestic icebergs calving from Vatnajökull glacier and serenely floating on the lagoon's waters. Take a boat tour through the glistening ice giants, paddle a kayak amongst the icy sculptures, or marvel at Diamond Beach, where icebergs wash ashore like frozen jewels.

As of the writing of this book, the site is open 24 hours a day, every day.

Jökulsárlón Glacier Lagoon.

Justraveling.com, CC BY-SA 4.0 <https://creativecommons.org/licenses/by-sa/4.0>, via Wikimedia Commons: https://commons.wikimedia.org/wiki/File:J%C3%B6kuls%C3%A1rl%C3%B3n_Glacier_Lagoon.jpg

- **Seljalandsfoss and Gljúfrabúi Waterfalls:** Step behind the thundering curtain of Seljalandsfoss waterfall for a unique perspective. Hike further to discover its hidden twin, Gljúfrabúi, nestled within a cave and pulsating with raw power.

As of the writing of this book, the site is open 24 hours a day, every day.

Seljalandsfoss waterfall.
Jakub Hałun, CC BY-SA 4.0 <https://creativecommons.org/licenses/by-sa/4.0>, via Wikimedia Commons: https://commons.wikimedia.org/wiki/File:Seljalandsfoss,_Iceland,_20230501_1328_3937.jpg

- **Skógafoss Waterfall:** Feel the earth tremble and the spray on your face as the mighty Skógafoss cascades down over 60 meters, rainbows arcing through the mist. Climb the staircase alongside the falls for breathtaking views and access to hiking trails leading to glaciers and volcanoes.

As of the writing of this book, the site is open 24 hours a day, every day.

Skógafoss Waterfall.
Jakub Hałun, CC BY-SA 4.0 <https://creativecommons.org/licenses/by-sa/4.0>, via Wikimedia Commons: https://commons.wikimedia.org/wiki/File:Sk%C3%B3gafoss,_Iceland,_20230501_1444_3968.jpg

- **Svartifoss Waterfall:** Hike through the dramatic basalt columns of Skaftafell National Park to reach Svartifoss, a majestic black waterfall framed by volcanic rock. Its dark beauty offers a stark contrast to the turquoise glacial waters.

As of the writing of this book, the site is open 24 hours a day, every day.

Svartifoss Waterfall.
Spike, CC BY-SA 4.0 <https://creativecommons.org/licenses/by-sa/4.0>, via Wikimedia Commons: https://commons.wikimedia.org/wiki/File:Svartifoss_Panorama_01.jpg

- **Reynisdrangar Sea Stacks:** Gaze upon the Reynisdrangar sea stacks, basalt giants rising from the ocean like petrified trolls guarding the black sand beach. Visit during storms to witness the ocean's fury against these stoic rock sentinels.

As of the writing of this book, the the site is open 24 hours a day, every day.

Reynisdrangar sea stacks.
Jakub Fryš, CC BY-SA 4.0 <https://creativecommons.org/licenses/by-sa/4.0>, via Wikimedia Commons: https://commons.wikimedia.org/wiki/File:Reynisdrangar_basalt_rocks.jpg

- **Raufarholshellir Lava Tunnel**: Journey into the earth's fiery past at Raufarholshellir, a vast lava cave adorned with colorful formations. Guided tours take you through tunnels carved by ancient lava flows, revealing a hidden world of volcanic wonder.

As of the writing of this book, the normal opening hours are 9 AM to 5 PM, every day, but please double-check the opening hours online should there have been any slight change in their schedule.

Raufarholshellir lava tunnel.
Jakub Hałun, CC BY-SA 4.0 <https://creativecommons.org/licenses/by-sa/4.0>, via Wikimedia Commons: https://commons.wikimedia.org/wiki/File:Raufarh%C3%B3lshellir,_Iceland,_20230502_1300_4213.jpg

- **Eldhraun Lava Field:** Hike across the vast and desolate Eldhraun lava field, a stark reminder of the 934-938 eruption that spewed lava for six years. Explore craters and lava tubes and feel the weight of geological time beneath your feet.

As of the writing of this book, the site is open 24 hours a day, every day.

Eldhraun lava field.
todd.vision, CC BY 2.0 <https://creativecommons.org/licenses/by/2.0>, via Wikimedia Commons: https://commons.wikimedia.org/wiki/File:Eldhraun_lava_field_(43111363612).jpg

- **Skógar Museum:** Delve into the past at the Skógar Museum, with exhibits showing the region's maritime history, farming traditions, and folklore. Explore the traditional turf houses and learn about the lives of those who braved the South Coast's wild beauty.

As of the writing of this book, the normal opening hours are 10 AM to 5 PM. They are open every day except for the 24th and 25th of December and the first of January. Please double-check the opening hours online should there have been any slight change in their schedule.

Skógar Museum.
Sally Wilson, CC BY-SA 2.0 <https://creativecommons.org/licenses/by-sa/2.0>, via Wikimedia Commons: https://commons.wikimedia.org/wiki/File:Skogar_Folk_Museum_(9503321868).jpg

- **Heiðmörk Nature Reserve:** Escape the crowds and explore the diverse landscapes of Heiðmörk, Iceland's largest forest reserve. Hike through geothermal areas, bike along scenic trails, and discover hidden waterfalls in the midst of lush vegetation.

As of the writing of this book, the site is open 24 hours a day, every day of the week.

- **Seltún Geothermal Area:** Hike through a colorful wonderland of boiling mud pools, steaming vents, and vibrant hot springs in this active geothermal zone. Lose yourself in the otherworldly landscape and breathe in the sulfurous air as the earth bubbles and gurgles around you.

Seltún geothermal area.
Ainars Brūvelis, CC BY-SA 3.0 <https://creativecommons.org/licenses/by-sa/3.0>, via Wikimedia Commons:
https://commons.wikimedia.org/wiki/File:Seltun,_geothermal_area_Kr%C3%BDsuv%C3%ADk_-_panoramio.jpg

Transport:
- **Car Rental:** The best way to explore the South Coast at your own pace and reach hidden gems. Several rental agencies offer pick-up and drop-off at Keflavík airport or Reykjavík.
- **South Coast Day Tours:** Numerous tour operators offer organized trips from Reykjavík, covering highlights with guides and transportation. Ideal for those without a car or short on time.
- **Public Bus:** Strætó buses connect some key South Coast destinations, although flexibility is limited compared to other options.

Did You Know: The legendary Katla volcano, slumbering beneath Mýrdalsjökull glacier, is one of Iceland's most active, erupting on average every 60 years. Local folklore paints it as the gateway to Hell, guarded by the fearsome fire giant Surtr.

Experiences:

- **Northern Lights Chase:** During winter months, when emerald and turquoise lights dance across the night sky, embark on a guided tour from Jökulsárlón or Vik to witness the mesmerizing aurora borealis. Escape light pollution, wait patiently under the starlit expanse, and be awestruck by the celestial light show reflected on the glacier lagoon or black sand beach.
- **Ice Climbing and Glacier Hiking:** Feel the thrill of scaling the icy slopes of Vatnajökull glacier with experienced guides. These adrenaline-pumping adventures offer unique perspectives of the glacial world and a profound connection with Iceland's icy heart.
- **Horseback Riding on Black Sand Beaches:** Experience the South Coast's wild beauty from a different perspective on horseback. Gallop along the black sand beaches near Vík, feeling the wind in your hair and the rhythmic beat of hooves against the volcanic sand.
- **Reykjadalur Hot Spring Valley:** Hike through a geothermal wonderland in Reykjadalur Valley, where steam vents hiss and hot springs bubble amidst colorful mountains. Take a dip in natural pools carved into the earth, feeling the warmth embrace your body and the stress melt away.

Did You Know: Heiðmörk Nature Reserve, once a royal hunting ground, was gifted to the Icelandic people in 1907. Legend tells of outlaws hiding in the reserve's forests and caves, adding an air of mystique to its verdant slopes.

Family Fun:

- **Lava Tunnel Raufarhólshellir:** Families with adventurous spirits will love exploring the Raufarhólshellirlava tunnel. Children will be amazed by the colorful formations and stories of volcanic eruptions, making it an educational and exciting adventure.
- **Seljalandsfoss Waterfall:** Behind the Falls tour is a thrilling experience for older children. Walk behind the cascading curtain of water, feel the spray, and marvel at the natural power of the

falls from a unique perspective.

- **Vík Horse Adventure:** Take your children on a horse ride on the black sand beach of Vík with Vík Horse Adventure. Explore the surrounding countryside, learn about horsemanship traditions, and watch these gentle animals in their natural habitat.
- **Skaftafell Ice Cave Tour:** Experience the magic of an ice cave with a family-friendly guided tour. Explore the icy tunnels carved by melting glaciers, marvel at the cathedral-like chambers, and learn about the formation of these natural wonders.

Where to Eat:

- **Jökulsárlón Glacier Lagoon Restaurant:** Savor gourmet seafood and lamb dishes overlooking the breathtaking Jökulsárlón lagoon. Enjoy panoramic views of icebergs while indulging in fresh local cuisine.
- **Salthusid Restaurant:** This cozy restaurant near Vík offers a taste of Icelandic tradition with modern twists. Sample the lamb stew, the pan-fried fish, or the vegetarian options, all paired with local beers or wines.
- **Fjörubord Restaurant:** Located in Skógar, Fjörubord offers a delightful menu featuring locally sourced ingredients and stunning ocean views. Try the lobster soup, the grilled langoustine, or the lamb shoulder, all prepared with passion and fresh flavors.
- **Efstidalur Guesthouse and Restaurant:** Nestled near Seljalandsfoss, this family-run establishment offers authentic Icelandic cuisine with a warm atmosphere. Enjoy the lamb burger, the homemade skyr cake, or the traditional fish and chips, perfect for a post-waterfall adventure.

Shopping Guide:

- **Jökulsárlón Glacier Lagoon Ice Cave Shop:** Pick up a unique souvenir from your Jökulsárlón experience at the Ice Cave Shop. Find jewelry made from volcanic ash, glacial ice fragments, and Icelandic wool sweaters, each piece infused with the South Coast's spirit.
- **Skógar Museum Shop:** Support local artisans and discover Icelandic treasures at the Skógar Museum Shop. Browse hand-knitted wool sweaters, volcanic rock jewelry, and traditional

Icelandic crafts, each item carrying a story of the region's heritage.

- **Vík Wool Factory:** Immerse yourself in the world of Icelandic wool at the Vík Wool Factory. Watch local artisans spinning and weaving, purchase hand-knitted sweaters, blankets, and accessories, and experience the warmth and quality of Icelandic wool firsthand.
- **The Icelandic Store:** Located in various outlets across the South Coast, The Icelandic Store offers a vast selection of Icelandic souvenirs, from food products and volcanic rock jewelry to unique design items and wool sweaters. Pick up a piece of Iceland to take home with you and cherish the memories of your South Coast adventure.

Did You Know: Jökulsárlón glacier lagoon, formed by melting ice tongues, was featured in the James Bond film "Die Another Day," forever linking its icy beauty to Hollywood glamour.

Accommodations:

- **Sólheimasandur Guesthouse**: Nestled near Reynisdrangar sea stacks, Sólheimasandur Guesthouse offers modern comfort with breathtaking black sand beach views. Relax in the hot tub after a day of exploration, savor delicious meals in the onsite restaurant, and let the sound of crashing waves lull you to sleep.
- **Fosshotel Glacier Lagoon**: Enjoy contemporary style with glacier lagoon views at Fosshotel Glacier Lagoon. This modern hotel offers comfortable rooms, a cozy hot tub, and a restaurant serving fresh local cuisine, making it the perfect base for exploring Jökulsárlón and its icy wonders.
- **Skógafoss Guesthouse:** Experience Icelandic hospitality at Skógafoss Guesthouse, offering cozy rooms and traditional home-cooked meals within walking distance of the majestic Skógafoss waterfall. Relax in the communal living area, share stories with fellow travelers, and soak in the authentic atmosphere of a family-run guesthouse.
- **Skaftafell Basecamp:** Immerse yourself in the wilderness at Skaftafell Basecamp, which offers various accommodation options, from cabins and tents to campervans. Situated amidst the National Park's stunning landscapes, this eco-friendly campsite provides a perfect base for glacier hikes, ice cave explorations, and breathtaking scenery.

Sports and Leisure:
- **Hiking and Trekking:** The South Coast offers endless hiking trails for all levels, from short coastal walks to challenging glacier treks. Hike to the top of Skógafoss for panoramic views, explore the otherworldly landscapes of Skaftafell National Park, or conquer the Laugavegur Trail, a renowned multi-day trek through volcanic plains and geothermal valleys.
- **Kayaking and Boat Tours:** Glide across the glacial waters of Jökulsárlón lagoon, witnessing icebergs up close and marveling at the turquoise reflections. Guided kayak tours allow for intimate exploration, while boat tours offer panoramic views and informative commentary.
- **Caving and Canyoning:** Venture into the earth's hidden wonders with guided caving tours in Raufarhólshelliror Katla Geopark. Experienced adventurers can tackle canyoning adventures in hidden gorges, rappelling down waterfalls and navigating through the raw beauty of the South Coast's interior.
- **Scuba Diving and Snorkeling:** Dive into the icy depths of Silfra fissure near Þingvellir National Park, experiencing the underwater world where tectonic plates meet. Snorkeling tours in glacial lagoons offer encounters with icebergs and stunning underwater landscapes.

This comprehensive guide to Reykjanes Peninsula and the South Coast provides a treasure trove of information for travelers seeking to unravel its beauty. From awe-inspiring waterfalls and glacial wonders to hidden caves and volcanic landscapes, these Icelandic places promise an unforgettable symphony of fire and ice. Pack your hiking boots, embrace the elements, and prepare to be captivated by the raw magic of Iceland.

Chapter 5: Western Iceland

In the West Fjords, where the wind whispers tales of Viking sagas and waves crash against volcanic shores, lies a land painted in shades of moss green, glacier blue, and fiery black. This is Western Iceland, Sagaland, a region where ancient words echo in windswept valleys and breathtaking landscapes unfold at every turn. Here, glaciers carve their icy paths through moss-carpeted mountains, waterfalls thunder into the sea, and volcanoes slumber beneath brooding skies.

Step into a world where Egil Skallagrímsson's saga unfolds amidst dramatic fjords, where Laxdæla Saga whispers secrets from coastal cliffs, and where Eyrbyggja Saga comes alive in rugged landscapes etched by time. Western Iceland is more than just geography. It's a living tapestry woven from history, myth, and raw natural beauty. So, open your heart to the stories whispered by the wind, lace up your hiking boots, and prepare to be captivated by the wild symphony of Sagaland.

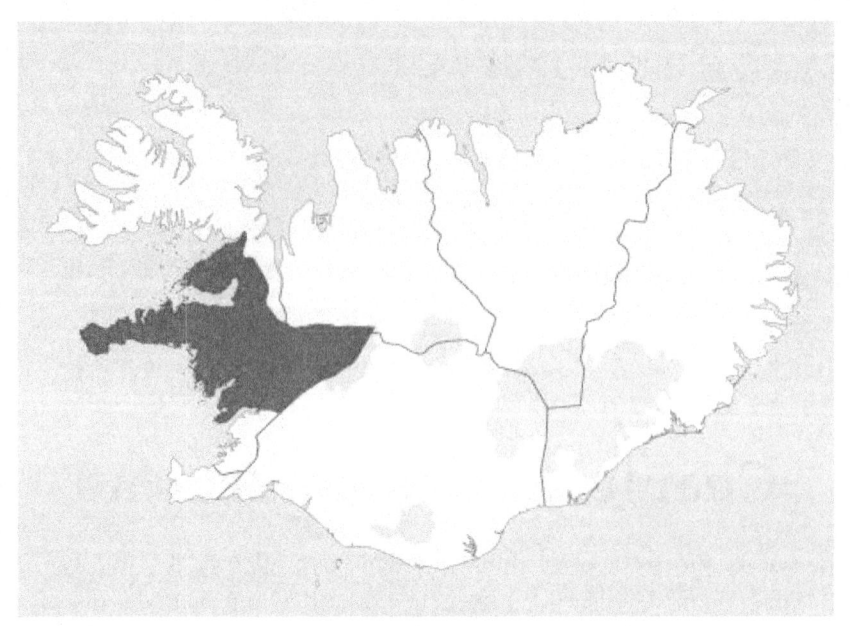

West Iceland.
TUBS, CC BY-SA 3.0 <https://creativecommons.org/licenses/by-sa/3.0>, via Wikimedia Commons, https://commons.wikimedia.org/wiki/File:Vesturland_in_Iceland.svg

Iceland in Miniature: Unveiling the Magic of Snæfellsnes Peninsula

Snæfellsnes Peninsula, affectionately nicknamed "Iceland in Miniature," is a jewel tucked away on the west coast. This 90-kilometer stretch of land holds a microcosm of everything Iceland has to offer, from volcanic peaks draped in glaciers to dramatic coastlines carved by waves. It's a landscape that whispers tales of Viking sagas and Jules Verne's sci-fi adventures, where waterfalls thunder and lava fields stretch like petrified waves.

Historical Background:

Snæfellsnes played a vital role in Iceland's early history. Viking settlers first stepped ashore here in the 9th century, drawn by its fertile lands and abundant fisheries. The region served as a setting for legendary sagas like "Eyrbyggja Saga" and "Grettis Saga," weaving its landscape into the tapestry of Icelandic folklore.

Did You Know: Djúpalónssandur, a black sand beach, owes its dramatic beauty to a tragic shipwreck in 1768, claimed by a rogue wave. Legend tells of the "Draugar," restless souls forever searching for lost oars amongst the pebbles.

Main Attractions:

- **Snæfellsjökull National Park:** Hike through rugged volcanic landscapes, breathe in the crisp glacial air, and marvel at the Snæfellsjökull glacier, shimmering like a diamond on the horizon. Explore lava fields, craters, and hidden waterfalls within the park's diverse terrain.

  As of the writing of this book, the normal opening hours are open 24 hours every day.

  Snæfellsjökull National Park.
  Markus Trienke, CC BY-SA 2.0 <https://creativecommons.org/licenses/by-sa/2.0>, via Wikimedia Commons: https://commons.wikimedia.org/wiki/File:Sn%C3%A6fellsj%C3%B6kull_National_Park_banner_1.jpg

- **Arnarstapi and Hellnar:** These charming coastal villages, nestled beneath towering cliffs, offer a glimpse into the peninsula's fishing heritage. Wander winding paths, gaze at natural rock arches, and explore hidden coves teeming with bird life.

  Arnarsrapi.
  Jakub Hałun, CC BY-SA 4.0 <https://creativecommons.org/licenses/by-sa/4.0>, via Wikimedia Commons: https://commons.wikimedia.org/wiki/File:Sea_cliff,_Arnarstapi,_Iceland,_20230505_1216_5168.jpg

- **Búðir Black Church (Búðakirkja):** A lone black church standing stark against the rugged shoreline, Búðir is a poignant symbol of resilience against the elements. Soak in the dramatic views and contemplate the mysteries whispered by the wind.

  As of the writing of this book, the church is closed. However, please double-check the opening hours online should there have been any slight change in their schedule.

  Búðir Black Church.
  Jakub Hałun, CC BY-SA 4.0 <https://creativecommons.org/licenses/by-sa/4.0>, via Wikimedia Commons: https://commons.wikimedia.org/wiki/File:B%C3%BA%C3%B0akirkja,_Iceland,_20230505_1030_5034.jpg

- **Vatnshellir and Sönghellir Lava Caves:** Embark on a subterranean adventure in these vast lava caves carved by ancient flows. Witness colorful formations and shimmering lava stalactites and feel the weight of geological time above you.

  As of the writing of this book, the normal opening hours for the Varnshellir lava cave is every dat from 10 AM to 6 PM, but please double-check the opening hours online should there have been any slight change in their schedule. Sönghellir is open 24 hours.

- **Djúpalónssandur Black Sand Beach:** Walk along the vast expanse of Djúpalónssandur, where black sand meets crashing waves. Climb the basalt cliffs for breathtaking panoramas, search for the legendary Draugr's oars, and feel the raw power of the ocean.

Djúpalónssandur Black Sand Beach.
Rob Oo from NL, CC BY 2.0 <https://creativecommons.org/licenses/by/2.0>, via Wikimedia Commons:
https://commons.wikimedia.org/wiki/File:Dj%C3%BApal%C3%B3nssandur_(14453228065).jpg

- **Kirkjufell Mountain and Kirkjufellsfossar Waterfall:** This iconic duo, made famous by Game of Thrones, offers mesmerizing beauty. Hike to the top of Kirkjufell for panoramic views, capture the cascading Kirkjufellsfossar waterfall in your lens, and soak in the otherworldly landscapes.

Kirkjufell Mountain.
Beardhatcode, CC0, via Wikimedia Commons:
https://commons.wikimedia.org/wiki/File:Kirkjufell_in_winter.jpg

- **Stykkishólmur:** Explore this charming island town connected to the mainland by a bridge. Wander through colorful houses, sample fresh seafood at the harbor, and climb the Guðlaugur Lookout for stunning vistas.

Stykkishólmur.
Balise42, CC BY-SA 4.0 <https://creativecommons.org/licenses/by-sa/4.0>, via Wikimedia Commons: https://commons.wikimedia.org/wiki/File:View_of_Stykkish%C3%B3lmur.jpg

- **Borgarnes Settlement Center:** Delve into Iceland's Viking past at the Borgarnes Settlement Center. Discover archaeological finds, learn about the region's early settlers, and stand on the very spot where Iceland's first Alþingi convened.

As of the writing of this book, the normal opening hours are every day from 10 AM to 9 PM, but please double-check the opening hours online should there have been any slight change in their schedule.

Transport:

- **Car Rental:** The best way to explore Snæfellsnes at your own pace, reaching hidden gems and off-the-beaten-path sights. Several rental agencies offer pick-up and drop-off at Keflavík airport or Reykjavík.
- **Snæfellsnes Day Tours:** Numerous tour operators offer organized trips from Reykjavík, covering highlights with guides and transportation. Ideal for those without a car or short on time.

- **Public Bus:** Strætó buses connect some key points on the peninsula, although flexibility is limited compared to other options.

Did You Know: Snæfellsjökull glacier, crowned the peninsula's crown jewel, served as the gateway to the Earth's core in Jules Verne's "Journey to the Center of the Earth."

Experiences:
- **Whale-Watching Tours:** Sail off the coast and witness the majestic giants of the ocean, including humpback whales and minke whales. These thrilling tours offer a glimpse into the marine life thriving in Icelandic waters.
- **Ice Cave Adventures:** Explore the hidden icy world beneath Snæfellsjökull glacier with guided tours. Traverse frozen tunnels, marvel at shimmering ice formations, and feel the chill of this glacial kingdom.
- **Snæfellsjökull Glacier Hike:** For experienced adventurers, conquer the ice slopes of Snæfellsjökull with guided glacier hikes. Experience the thrill of climbing on ice, witness breathtaking panoramas, and connect with the power of glacial landscapes.
- **Horseback Riding Tours:** Gallop along the black sand beaches, traverse rolling hills, and feel the wind in your hair with horseback riding tours. Explore the peninsula from a different perspective, bonding with these gentle Icelandic horses.
- **Northern Lights Photography Tours:** During winter months, when emerald and turquoise lights dance across the sky, embark on a guided photography tour to capture the mesmerizing aurora borealis. Escape light pollution, stand in awe of the celestial light show, and capture breathtaking images of the dancing lights above Snæfellsjökull.
- **Culinary Tour and Food Tastings:** Indulge in the freshest seafood, sample traditional Icelandic lamb dishes, and discover the peninsula's culinary delights with food tours and tastings. Visit local farms, learn about sustainable food practices, and savor the flavors of Snæfellsnes.

Family Fun:
- **Bjarnarfoss Waterfall:** This family-friendly walk leads to a stunning waterfall cascading into a turquoise pool. Explore the

surrounding volcanic rock formations, let the children build sandcastles on the black sand beach nearby, and enjoy a picnic surrounded by breathtaking scenery.
- **Saxhóll Crater:** Embark on a short hike to the rim of Saxhóll crater, a dormant volcano offering panoramic views of the surrounding landscapes. Let the children climb the volcanic slopes, imagine eruptions of the past, and learn about the power of geothermal forces.
- **Lýsuhólslaug Geothermal Pool:** Enjoy a dip in the warm waters of Lýsuhólslaug, a natural geothermal pool nestled in lava fields. This family-friendly option offers a unique and relaxing experience perfect for rejuvenating after a day of exploration.
- **Borgarnes Settlement Center:** Bring history to life for your children at the Settlement Center. Discover Viking artifacts, watch interactive exhibits, and let them dress up as Viking warriors, creating lasting memories of Iceland's early settlers.

Where to Eat:
- **Harbor House Café in Grundarfjordur:** Savor fresh seafood and lamb dishes with panoramic ocean views at Harbor House Café. Indulge in local delicacies like lobster soup, pan-fried fish, and traditional fish and chips, all prepared with fresh ingredients and Icelandic flair.
- **Búðakirkja Kaffihús at Búðir Black Church:** Enjoy a unique dining experience at this cafe housed within the historic Búðir Black Church. Savor homemade soups, sandwiches, and traditional Icelandic pastries, soaking in the dramatic views and the church's timeless atmosphere.

Did You Know: The Vatnshellir lava cave was once used as a hideout by outlaws; its hidden chambers are rumored to hold buried treasures.

Shopping Guide:
- **Kidka Wool Factory:** Witness the art of Icelandic wool knitting firsthand at the Kidka Wool Factory. Pick up hand-knitted sweaters, hats, and accessories, each piece infused with Icelandic warmth and quality.
- **Settlement Center Shop in Borgarnes:** Find historical treasures and handmade Icelandic crafts at the Settlement Center Shop. Choose from Viking-themed jewelry, traditional knitted items,

and books on Icelandic history and culture.
- **The Icelandic Store:** Located in various outlets across the peninsula, The Icelandic Store offers a vast selection of Icelandic souvenirs, from volcanic rock jewelry and food products to unique design items and wool sweaters. Pick up a piece of Iceland to take home and cherish the memories of your Snæfellsnes adventure.

Entertainment:
- **Grundarfjörður Music Festival:** This annual festival held in July and August brings together Icelandic and international musicians for a vibrant celebration of music surrounded by stunning landscapes.
- **Snæfellsjökull National Park Ranger Talks:** Learn about the park's geology, wildlife, and cultural significance through guided ranger talks offered at various locations. Gain insights into the formation of glaciers, the unique flora and fauna of the region, and the stories woven into the landscape.
- **Búðakirkja Black Church Concerts:** Immerse yourself in the ethereal atmosphere of the Búðir Black Church during occasional concerts featuring Icelandic musicians. Witness the interplay of music and light within the historic church, creating an unforgettable experience.
- **Krýsuvík Geothermal Spa:** While not directly on the peninsula, a visit to the nearby Krýsuvík Geothermal Spa offers a unique and luxurious escape. Relax in hot tubs, steam rooms, and saunas fueled by geothermal energy, enjoying the rejuvenating benefits of Iceland's natural wonders.

Sports and Leisure:
- **Snæfellsjökull Ski Glacier:** Experience the thrill of skiing or snowboarding on the slopes of Snæfellsjökull glacier all year round. This unique opportunity offers breathtaking views and challenging runs for all levels of skiers and snowboarders.
- **Snæfellsnes Golf Course:** Enjoy a game of golf at the Snæfellsnes Golf Course with dramatic landscapes as a backdrop. This 18-hole course, carved into the volcanic terrain, offers stunning vistas and a unique golfing experience.
- **Snæfellsnes Horseback Riding Trails:** Explore the peninsula's

diverse terrain on horseback, choosing from leisurely coastal rides to challenging mountain trails. Connect with these gentle animals, witness hidden waterfalls and lava fields, and create memories that will last a lifetime.

- **Kayaking and Boat Tours:** See Snæfellsnes from a different perspective with kayaking or boat tours along the coast. Navigate hidden coves, paddle past towering cliffs, and encounter marine life like seals and whales in their natural habitat.
- **Snæfellsnes Hiking Trails:** Choose from a network of hiking trails ranging from easy coastal walks to challenging glacier treks. Explore lava fields, climb volcanic peaks, and discover hidden waterfalls, each step revealing the peninsula's breathtaking beauty.

Accommodations:

- **Bikers Paradise Hotel in Ólafsvík:** This modern hotel offers comfortable rooms with stunning ocean views. Enjoy the on-site restaurant serving local cuisine, relax in the hot tub, and take advantage of the hotel's tour booking services.
- **Fosshotel Hellnar in Hellnar:** This charming guesthouse provides cozy accommodations and a warm atmosphere. Savor delicious home-cooked meals, enjoy the surrounding nature, and unwind in the communal living area, perfect for meeting fellow travelers.
- **Vogur Country Lodge in Stykkishólmur:** Experience the charm of island living in these modern apartments overlooking the harbor. Enjoy self-catering facilities, stunning views, and easy access to the town's shops and restaurants.
- **Snæfellsnes Cottages and Cabins:** Immerse yourself in the peninsula's wilderness with a stay in a cozy cottage or cabin. Choose from various locations, wake up to breathtaking views, and enjoy the peace of the Icelandic countryside.

You have just had a glimpse into the magic of Snæfellsnes, discovering its diverse attractions, experiences, and accommodation options. Whether you seek adventure on glaciers or serenity by black sand beaches, Snæfellsnes has something for everyone.

Akranes: Where History Breathes and Whales Whisper Secrets

Just a stone's throw from Reykjavík's bustle, Akranes charms with coastal beauty and a whisper of Viking sagas. This idyllic town, bathed in golden sunsets and overlooking Faxaflói Bay, is a tapestry woven from history, dramatic scenery, and vibrant culture. So, adventurer, buckle up and explore Akranes' hidden gems.

Historical Background:

Akranes' whispers echo back to the 9th century when Viking settlers like Styrbjörn the Strong carved their names in the land. Fishing became its lifeblood, shaping its soul and leaving a legacy of weathered boats and hardy men. Today, Akranes embraces its past while looking towards the future, blending historical charm with modern spirit.

Main Attractions:

- **Akrafjall Mountain:** Hike to the summit for breathtaking panoramas for the perfect Instagram shot.

Akrafjall Mountain.

Diego Delso, CC BY-SA 4.0 <https://creativecommons.org/licenses/by-sa/4.0>, via Wikimedia Commons: https://commons.wikimedia.org/wiki/File:Monta%C3%B1a_volc%C3%A1nica_Akrafjall,_Akranes,_Vesturland,_Islandia,_2014-08-14,_DD_004.JPG

- **Old Akranes Lighthouse:** Step back in time at this charming lighthouse, still guiding ships and housing a maritime history museum.

As of the writing of this book, the normal opening hours are Monday to Friday from 10 AM to 4 PM and Saturday and Sunday from 12 PM to 3 PM, but please double-check the opening hours online should there have been any slight change in their schedule.

Old Akranes Lighthouse.
Diego Delso, CC BY-SA 4.0 <https://creativecommons.org/licenses/by-sa/4.0>, via Wikimedia Commons: https://commons.wikimedia.org/wiki/File:Antiguo_faro_de_Akranes,_Vesturland,_Islandia,_2014-08-14,_DD_008.JPG

- **Akranes Folk Museum:** Discover Viking artifacts, traditional fishing practices, and intricate handicrafts, experiencing the town's soul through objects and stories.

As of the writing of this book, the normal opening hours from May 15th to September 14th are every day from 11 AM to 5 PM and from September 15th to May 14th they are open only on Saturdays from 1 PM to 5 PM. Please double-check the opening hours online should there have been any slight change in their schedule.

- **Hvalfjörður Tunnel:** Drive through the world's longest underwater tunnel, emerging on the other side, ready for fresh adventures.

- **Glymur Waterfall:** Hike through Hvalfjörður's splendor to reach Glymur, Iceland's highest cascade. Feel the thunder of water plunging 198 meters, inhaling the crisp air and soaking in nature's raw power.

As of the writing of this book, the site is open 24 hours a day, every day.

Glymur Waterfall.
https://commons.wikimedia.org/wiki/File:Glymur_pan_1-10-08.JPG

Transport:
- **Car Rental:** Explore at your own pace with rentals available at Keflavík airport or Reykjavík.
- **Strætó Buses:** Public buses connect Akranes to Reykjavík and surrounding towns, offering a budget-friendly option.
- **Organized Tours:** Day trips from Reykjavík cover key attractions with guides and transportation, ideal for those short on time.

Did You Know: World War II saw Akranes host a US military base, leaving behind "Camp Brauterholt," an eerie reminder of the past.

Experiences:
- **Whale Watching Tours**: Embark from Akranes Harbor and witness the majestic giants of the ocean breaching, gliding, and playing alongside the boat.
- **Lava Tunnel Exploration**: Journey into Víðgelmir Cave, a vast lava tunnel formed by ancient eruptions. Marvel at colorful formations, learn about volcanic history, and feel the eerie stillness of the subterranean world.
- **Akranes Saltfisk Festival**: Immerse yourself in culinary heritage at the annual Saltfisk Festival in February. Sample traditional salted fish dishes, watch cooking demonstrations, and participate in cultural events celebrating the town's maritime roots.
- **Midnight Sun Hikes**: During summer, experience the magic of the midnight sun with exhilarating hikes on Akrafjall Mountain. Witness the sky blaze with hues of orange and pink, painting the landscape in a surreal glow.
- **Viking Sagas Come Alive**: Embark on a guided walking tour through Akranes, retracing the steps of Viking settlers and immersing yourself in the town's ancient sagas. Learn about Styrbjörn the Strong, explore historical sites like the old harbor and the church ruins, and let your imagination paint vivid pictures of the past.
- **Geocaching Adventures:** Turn Akranes into a treasure hunt with geocaching, a family-friendly activity that blends exploration, technology, and discovery. Download the geocaching app, follow clues hidden around town, and uncover hidden caches containing trinkets and stories.
- **Akranes Art Trail:** Discover hidden gems of public art scattered throughout the town. From murals on buildings to sculptures nestled in parks, this self-guided art tour offers a unique perspective on Akranes and its creative spirit.

Family Fun:
- **Akranes Folk Museum:** The Akranes Folk Museum provides a unique insight into the history of Akranes and its surrounding area. The exhibition reflects living conditions, life at sea and in rural areas, as well as the way people in Akranes live. Enjoy learning about the history of this interesting area through an

immersive experience.
- **Akranes Swimming Pool:** Take a refreshing dip in the Akranes swimming pool, featuring geothermal hot tubs, a waterslide, and a children's pool. Enjoy family time surrounded by stunning fjord scenery, splashing and relaxing under the Icelandic sky.
- **Glymur Waterfall Hike (For Older Children):** Embark on a family adventure to the foot of Glymur Waterfall. This moderate hike through scenic Hvalfjörður rewards with breathtaking views and the awe-inspiring power of Iceland's highest cascade.

Did You Know: Akranes is the birthplace of Sigur Rós, whose haunting melodies seem to emanate from the town's soul.

Where to Eat:
- **Bryggjan Brugghus:** Savor fresh seafood with stunning harbor views at Bryggjan Brugghus. Sample the catch of the day, indulge in traditional Icelandic lamb stew, or try the local fish and chips, all prepared with fresh ingredients and a touch of Icelandic flair.
- **Lighthouse Restaurant:** Experience Akranes' culinary heritage at the Lighthouse Restaurant, specializing in traditional salted fish dishes. Try the dried fish with potatoes and butter, the smoked salmon, or the fish soup, each bite bursting with history and local flavors.
- **Kallabakarí:** Grab a sweet treat or a light lunch at Kallabakarí, a cozy bakery known for its delicious pastries and bread. Indulge in cinnamon rolls, freshly baked croissants, or a traditional Icelandic "kleinur" pastry, perfect for a quick energy boost.

Shopping Guide:
- **Akranes Folk Museum Shop:** Find unique souvenirs and handcrafted treasures at the Folk Museum Shop. Pick up hand-knitted wool sweaters, traditional Icelandic jewelry, or historical books, each item infused with the spirit of Akranes' past.
- **Saltfiskstofa Shop**: Taste Akranes home with you from the Saltfiskstofa Shop. Browse salted fish products, local jams and chutneys, and Icelandic spices, perfect for recreating the town's culinary magic in your kitchen.
- **Akranes Art and Crafts Market:** Immerse yourself in local creativity at the Akranes Art & Crafts Market, which is held during the summer months. Discover handmade jewelry,

paintings, sculptures, and other artistic treasures, each piece capturing the essence of Akranes' vibrant spirit.

Did You Know: A tragic whale beaching in 2010 sparked conversations about animal welfare and environmental conservation.

Sports and Leisure:

- **Akranes Golf Course:** Challenge yourself on the 18-hole Akranes Golf Course, offering stunning fjord views and a unique golfing experience amid volcanic landscapes.
- **Horseback Riding Tours:** Explore Akranes' scenic coastline and rolling hills on horseback with guided tours. Connect with these gentle animals, witness hidden coves and lava fields, and create memories that will last a lifetime.
- **Kayaking and Boat Tours:** Paddle along the Akranes coastline or sail across Faxaflói Bay, discovering hidden coves, spotting marine life, and enjoying the tranquility of the sea. Choose from leisurely tours to thrilling adventures, all offering unique perspectives on the town.

Accommodations:

- **Hotel Laxarbakki:** Choose modern comfort and stunning views of River Laxá at Hotel Laxarbakki. Relax in the spa, enjoy delicious meals at the on-site restaurant, and explore the town from this convenient location.
- **Móar Cottage:** Experience Icelandic hospitality at the Akranes Guesthouse, which offers comfortable rooms and a warm atmosphere. Savor home-cooked meals in the communal dining area, share stories with fellow travelers, and feel the charm of local life in this inviting guesthouse.

Whether you seek adventure on Glymur Falls, serenity by the fjords, or a taste of Akranes' cultural heritage, this coastal town offers something for everyone. Pack your sense of adventure, lace up your boots, and prepare to be captivated by the charm of Akranes, where history whispers, whales dance on the waves, and nature paints breathtaking landscapes that will stay etched in your memories forever.

Dalir: Where Nature Whispers and Family Adventures Await

Nestled in the rugged beauty of West Iceland, Dalir unveils a wonderland where time gently slows. This picturesque region, centered around the charming village of Búðardalur, beckons families and nature lovers alike with its thermal springs, idyllic landscapes, and rich cultural heritage. It's time to uncover the magic of Dalir, where every corner offers a new adventure.

Historical Background:

The saga of Dalir whispers back through the centuries, etched in Viking folklore and Laxdæla saga's dramatic tales. Vikings like Eiríkur rauði Þorvaldsson, father of Leif Eiriksson, once roamed these lands, leaving behind memories of their exploits in place names and ancient ruins. Through the ages, generations of farmers and fishermen carved their lives out of the rugged terrain, shaping a culture of resilience and hospitality that lingers today.

Main Attractions:

- **Guðrúnarlaug Hot Spring:** Dive into the milky blue waters of this natural geothermal pool, hidden amongst moss-covered hills. Let the hot spring's healing powers rejuvenate your body and soul as you soak in the serene mountain air.

As of the writing of this book, the site is open 24 hours a day, every day.

- **Erpsstaðir Dairy Farm:** Experience the warmth of Icelandic hospitality at Erpsstaðir Dairy Farm, a traditional working farm offering horseback riding, sheepdog demonstrations, and delicious homemade treats made with fresh local ingredients.

As of the writing of this book, the normal opening hours are every day from 1 PM to 5 PM, but please double-check the opening hours online should there have been any slight change in their schedule.

- **Ljárskógar and Sólheimar Lakes:** Discover tranquil beauty at Ljárskógar and Sólheimar lakes, perfect for strolls, birdwatching, or picnicking surrounded by serene landscapes.

As of the writing of this book, you can visit the lakes at any time of the day, any day of the week, but please double-check the opening hours online should there have been any slight change in their schedule.

- **Búðardalur Village:** Explore the charming village of Búðardalur, with its colorful houses, quaint shops, and welcoming atmosphere. Sample local delicacies, browse for handcrafted souvenirs, and soak in the authentic Icelandic vibe.

As of the writing of this book, the normal opening hours are Tuesday to Thursday from 10 AM to 6 PM and Saturday from 10 AM to 4 PM, they are closed on Sundays and Monday. Please double-check the opening hours online should there have been any slight change in their schedule.

Transport:
- **Car Rental:** Explore Dalir at your own pace with a car rental from Keflavík airport or Reykjavík.
- **Strætó Buses:** Public buses connect Dalir to surrounding towns, offering a budget-friendly option.
- **Organized Tours:** Day trips from Reykjavík cover key attractions with guides and transportation, ideal for those short on time.

Did You Know: Dalir is famous for its unique cheese, Dala Auður, named after the legendary Viking warrior woman Auður djúpaúdga Ketilsdóttir.

Experiences:
- **Viking Sagas Come Alive:** Embark on a guided tour at Eiríksstaðir, where history comes alive as you delve into the lives of Viking settlers. Dress in traditional garb, witness demonstrations of ancient crafts, and feel the spirit of Viking warriors come alive.
- **Glacier Walks:** Embark on a thrilling adventure onto Snæfellsjökull glacier, experiencing the raw power and beauty of Iceland's icy giants. Explore crevasses and ice caves and feel the exhilaration of walking in another world.
- **Dalir Folk Festival:** Immerse yourself in Icelandic culture at the annual Dalir Folk Festival, held during summer. Enjoy traditional music, dance performances, storytelling, and local culinary delights, celebrating the region's rich heritage.

Family Fun:
- **Lava Tunnel Exploration:** Journey into Víðgelmir Cave, a vast lava tunnel formed by ancient eruptions. Marvel at colorful formations, learn about volcanic history, and feel the eerie stillness of the subterranean world.
- **Dalir Children's Farm:** Let little ones experience the joys of farm life at the Dalir Children's Farm. Pet-friendly animals, hayrides, and pony rides ensure endless hours of fun and learning for the whole family.
- **Geothermal Pool Fun:** Splash and play at the Búðardalur swimming pool, featuring indoor and outdoor geothermal pools, a waterslide, and a children's area. Enjoy family time amidst stunning fjord scenery, making memories that will last a lifetime.

Did You Know: Eiríksstaðir, the former homestead of Eirίkr Þorvaldsson, is a reconstructed Viking longhouse near Búðardalur, and offers a glimpse into the everyday life of these legendary explorers.

Where to Eat:
- **Blómalindin Kaffihornid:** Grab a quick bite or a delicious pastry at Blómalindin Kaffihornid, a cozy spot in the heart of the village. Sample homemade soups and sandwiches, savor cinnamon rolls or freshly baked bread, and soak in the warm atmosphere.
- **Erpsstaðir Dairy Farm Restaurant:** Experience the true taste of Dalir at the Erpsstaðir dairy farm restaurant. Savor traditional Icelandic dishes like smoked lamb, lamb stew with potatoes, or homemade skyr, all made with fresh farm ingredients following recipes that have been passed down through generations.

Shopping Guide:
- **Bolli Icelandic Craft in Búðardalur:** Find unique souvenirs and handcrafted treasures at Bolli Icelandic Craf. Pick up hand-knitted wool sweaters, Icelandic jewelry made with volcanic stones, or traditional wood carvings, each piece infused with the spirit of Dalir's creativity.
- **Erpsstaðir Dairy Farm Shop:** Taste the farm home with you from the Erpsstaðir Dairy Farm Shop. Browse delicious cheeses like Dala Auður, homemade jams and chutneys, and locally sourced wool products, perfect for recreating the flavors and warmth of Dalir in your kitchen.

- **Dalir Book Shop:** Immerse yourself in Icelandic literature and local stories at the Dalir Book Shop. Discover novels by renowned Icelandic authors, children's books featuring adorable Icelandic animals, and historical books on the region's rich Viking heritage.

Did You Know: The region was once home to numerous hot springs, but legend tells of a mischievous troll who hid them all except for the magical Guðrúnarlaug.

Sports and Leisure:
- **Dalir Golf Course:** Challenge yourself on the 9-hole Dalir Golf Course, offering stunning lake and mountain views. Enjoy a peaceful round surrounded by nature, perfect for golfers of all levels.
- **Kayaking and Boat Tours:** Explore Dalir's coastline and serene lakes from a different perspective with kayaking or boat tours. Paddle through picturesque landscapes, spot seabirds and seals, and enjoy the tranquility of the waters.
- **Dalir Hiking Trails:** Choose from a network of hiking trails winding through Dalir's diverse terrain, from gentle lakeside walks to challenging mountain climbs. Witness hidden waterfalls, discover wildflowers in bloom, and inhale the fresh Icelandic air.
- **Birding:** Dalir is a haven for birdwatchers, with diverse species like puffins, guillemots, and Arctic terns calling the region home. Explore the coastlines, lakes, and mountains with your binoculars and capture the beauty of these feathered friends.

Accommodations:
- **The Castle Guesthouse:** Experience Icelandic hospitality at the Castle Guesthouse, offering cozy rooms and a warm atmosphere. Enjoy delicious home-cooked meals in the communal dining area, share stories with fellow travelers, and relax in the comfortable lounge area.
- **Dalakot Búðardal:** Immerse yourself in the peace of Dalir's countryside with a stay in a cozy cottage. Enjoy the privacy and comfort of your own space, wake up to the breathtaking mountain or lake views, and explore the surrounding natural wonders at your own pace.

- **Erpsstaðir Dairy Farm Accommodations:** Experience life on a working farm at Erpsstaðir Farm Accommodations. Choose from comfortable rooms or traditional turf houses, savor farm-to-table meals, and participate in farm activities like horseback riding and sheepdog demonstrations.

Western Iceland, with its thermal springs, idyllic landscapes, and rich cultural heritage, awaits your exploration. In this family-friendly haven, nature whispers and adventures unfold around every corner. Embrace the spirit of exploration and prepare to be captivated by Sagaland.

Chapter 6: The Westfjords

Welcome to the wild fringes of Iceland, where windswept cliffs cradle serene fjords, rugged mountains kiss the sea, and the echoes of Viking sagas linger in the mist. Brace yourself, for you embark on a journey to the Westfjords, a land unlike any other. Here, nature reigns supreme, carving dramatic fjords, sculpting volcanic peaks, and painting landscapes with strokes of emerald, sapphire, and obsidian.

Prepare to disconnect from the humdrum and reconnect with the untamed soul of Iceland, where the only crowds are seabirds, and the only traffic jam is a pod of playful whales. Tighten your boots, open your heart to the raw beauty, and lose yourself in the magic of the Westfjords.

The Westfjords.
A Red Cherry, CC BY-SA 4.0 <https://creativecommons.org/licenses/by-sa/4.0>, via Wikimedia Commons https://commons.wikimedia.org/wiki/File:Isafjordur.png

Westfjords: Where Untamed Beauty Meets Viking Whispers

Iceland's crown jewels may not glitter in the south, but in the remote northwestern corner – amidst the emerald fjords and jagged cliffs – lies a land where wilderness whispers Viking sagas and nature paints landscapes with strokes of breathtaking beauty. Welcome to the Westfjords, a haven for explorers, photographers, and those seeking an authentic Icelandic experience beyond the crowds.

Historical Background:

The Westfjords pulse with the rhythm of Viking sagas. Styrbjörn the Strong, a legendary figure whose name has been whispered through centuries, carved his name on this land, leaving behind remnants of ancient settlements and a spirit of resilience that persists to this day. Fishing villages sprung up in sheltered coves, their harbors echoing with stories of brave men and treacherous seas. Even the landscape carries history, shaped by volcanic eruptions and glaciers, a silent testament to the forces that forged this rugged paradise.

Main Attractions:

- **Ísafjörður:** Considered the honorary capital of the Westfjords, nestled amongst dramatic fjords, Ísafjörður offers cultural delights like the Westfjords Heritage Museum and cozy cafes alongside a buzzing harbor. Climb Ísafjörður Mountain for panoramic vistas or delve into the town's vibrant arts scene.

Ísafjörður.

Sturlast ~iswiki, CC BY-SA 4.0 <https://creativecommons.org/licenses/by-sa/4.0>, via Wikimedia Commons: https://commons.wikimedia.org/wiki/File:%C3%8Dsafj%C3%B6r%C3%B0ur_12_June_2019.jpg

- **Drangsnes Hot Pots:** Let the milky blue waters of these natural hot pools in Drangsnes soothe your soul and replenish your spirit, surrounded by volcanic landscapes. Hike nearby Bolafjall mountain for breathtaking summit views and soak in the tranquility of this hidden gem.

As of the writing of this book, the normal opening hours are every day from 9:30 AM to 6 PM, but please double-check the opening hours online should there have been any slight change in their schedule.

- **Grímsey Island:** Venture beyond the Arctic Circle to Grímsey Island, a remote outpost where life unfolds at a slower pace. Witness the midnight sun in summer, visit the island's charming church, and experience the unique culture of this isolated Icelandic community.

Grímsey Island.
MosheA, CC BY-SA 2.5 <https://creativecommons.org/licenses/by-sa/2.5>, via Wikimedia Commons: https://commons.wikimedia.org/wiki/File:Gr%C3%ADmsey_Iceland.JPG

- **Hornstrandir:** Hike through Hornstrandir, Europe's largest western wilderness reserve, where untouched beauty awaits your footsteps. Witness dramatic coastal cliffs, hidden valleys teeming with arctic flora, and a breathtaking sense of solitude. Explore abandoned villages and remnants of a bygone era and feel the weight of history in the untamed wilderness.

As of the writing of this book, the site is open every day, 24 hours a day.

Hornstrandir Waterfall.
Silverkey, CC BY-SA 3.0 <https://creativecommons.org/licenses/by-sa/3.0>, via Wikimedia Commons: https://commons.wikimedia.org/wiki/File:Hornstrandir_waterfall.jpg

- **The Icelandic Sea Monster Museum:** Unleash your inner child at this quirky museum in Bíldudalur, dedicated to the legends of Icelandic sea monsters. Discover intriguing exhibits, marvel at the "Stubbur," a massive tentacle that washed ashore in 1937, and let your imagination run wild with tales of krakens and sea serpents.

As of the writing of this book, the normal opening hours are every day from 10 AM to 6 PM, but please double-check the opening hours online should there have been any slight change in their schedule.

- **Dynjandi Waterfall:** Hike through scenic valleys and past cascading waterfalls until you reach the foot of Dynjandi, Iceland's sixth-highest waterfall. Feel the power of cascading water as it plunges 100 meters into a turquoise pool, creating a mesmerizing spectacle of nature's raw beauty.

Dynjandi waterfall.

Diego Delso, CC BY-SA 4.0 <https://creativecommons.org/licenses/by-sa/4.0>, via Wikimedia Commons: https://commons.wikimedia.org/wiki/File:Cascada_Dynjandi,_Vestfir%C3%B0ir,_Islandia,_2014-08-14,_DD_139-141_HDR.JPG

- **Látrabjarg:** Stand atop Europe's westernmost cliffs, Látrabjarg, and witness a kaleidoscope of seabird life. Puffins, razorbills, and guillemots paint the sky with their flights, forming a dense, cacophonous cloud against the rugged cliffs. Watch playful seals basking on the rocks below and breathe in the salty air, feeling invigorated by the wild energy of the coastline.

Látrabjarg.
https://commons.wikimedia.org/wiki/File:L%C3%A1trabjarg_Iceland.jpg

- **Þingeyrarkirkja:** Steeped in history, this stone church stands as a beacon of faith and resilience. Explore its unique architecture, delve into local history, and marvel at the craftsmanship that endured centuries of harsh weather.

As of the writing of this book, the normal opening hours are every day, from 10 AM to 5 PM, but please double-check the opening hours online should there have been any slight change in their schedule.

Þingeyrarkirkja.
Christian Bickel fingalo, CC BY-SA 2.0 DE <https://creativecommons.org/licenses/by-sa/2.0/de/deed.en>, via Wikimedia Commons:
https://commons.wikimedia.org/wiki/File:%C3%9Eingeyri_05.JPG

Transportation:
- **Car Rental:** Exploring the Westfjords at your own pace is best achieved with a car rental from Keflavík Airport or Reykjavík. Be prepared for winding roads and unpredictable weather, but the freedom and flexibility are unmatched.
- **Strætó Buses:** Public buses connect key towns and villages in the Westfjords, offering a budget-friendly option for travelers without a car. However, schedules can be limited, so plan your itinerary

accordingly.

- **Domestic Flights:** Regular flights connect Ísafjörður and Reykjavík, offering a convenient and scenic way to reach the Westfjords. This option is ideal for those short on time or seeking a bird's-eye view of the region's dramatic landscapes.

Did You Know: The Hornstrandir peninsula, dubbed "The Land of the Lost World," was once rumored to be inhabited by trolls and mythical creatures.

Experiences:

- **Arctic Fox Photography Tours:** Capture the elusive beauty of the Arctic fox, a symbol of the Westfjords' resilience, as it navigates the rugged terrain and adapts to the changes in its environment. The Arctic fox is known to be white; however, most don't know that the foxes' coat color changes to reflect the seasons! This is especially true for those found in Iceland, as only one-third will be seen in a white coat during the winter. The remaining two-thirds can mostly be seen with brown or grey coats, allowing them to blend in with the country's hillsides.
- **Horseback Riding Adventures:** Saddle up and explore the Westfjords on horseback, a traditional way to connect with the land and its history. Traverse coastal plains, trek through valleys dotted with wildflowers, and feel the thrill of riding along windswept cliffs, embracing the untamed spirit of the region.
- **Midnight Sun Hikes:** During summer, experience the surreal magic of the midnight sun on an unforgettable hike. Witness the landscape bathed in a golden glow as you ascend mountains or wander serene fjords, reveling in the endless daylight and the unique atmosphere of the Arctic summer.
- **Northern Lights Photography:** In winter, chase the dancing aurora borealis across the Westfjords' dark skies. Set up your camera amid snow-covered landscapes and capture the mesmerizing spectacle of emerald, violet, and turquoise ribbons swirling across the night sky, creating a celestial show like no other.
- **Glacier Kayak Tours:** Paddle alongside towering ice walls on a kayaking adventure and explore hidden coves carved by glaciers. Feel the chill of the icy waters, marvel at the intricate glacial formations, and gain a new perspective on the Westfjords' rugged

beauty from the vantage point of your kayak.

Did You Know: Vigur Island boasts the highest concentration of puffins in Iceland, offering a spectacle of colorful beaks and raucous calls.

Family Fun:

- **Whale-Watching Tours:** Embark on a thrilling whale-watching expedition from Ísafjörður or Húsavík and witness these majestic creatures gliding through the ocean. Spotting humpback whales breaching, playful dolphins, and curious minke whales creates lasting memories for the whole family.

- **Vatnsfjörður Nature Reserve:** Explore the vast Vatnsfjörður Nature Reserve, a land of diverse landscapes and rich animal life. Hike through birch forests, kayak on glistening lakes, and spot reindeer grazing on the windswept plains. Discover Viking remains and ancient burial mounds, telling stories of the region's past.

- **Rauðasandur (Red Sand Beach):** Let your inner child loose on the unique red sand beach of Rauðasandur. Feel the soft, crimson sand between your toes, marvel at the dramatic cliffs rising from the shore, and build sandcastles fit for giants. Hike to the nearby Rauðisandur hot springs for a relaxing dip in geothermal waters and complete the perfect family adventure.

Where to Eat:

- **Tjöruhúsið Restaurant (Ísafjörður):** Savor fresh seafood with breathtaking fjord views at Tjöruhúsið Restaurant. Indulge in the catch of the day, try the traditional Icelandic lamb stew, or sample the local smoked salmon, all prepared with fresh, local ingredients.

- **Kaffi Norðurfjörður (Drangsnes):** Enjoy a cozy atmosphere and homemade Icelandic fare at Kaffi Norðurfjörður. Warm up with a bowl of lamb soup, sample the traditional "kleinur" pastries, or indulge in a delicious fish and chips dish, all made with love and local ingredients.

Shopping Guide:

- **Handverk Húsið (Ísafjörður):** Find unique Icelandic souvenirs and handcrafted treasures at Handverk Húsið. Browse hand-knitted wool sweaters, jewelry made with volcanic stones, and traditional wood carvings, each piece infused with the spirit of

Westfjords craftsmanship.
- **Vatnsfjörður Visitor Center Shop:** Take a piece of the Vatnsfjörður Nature Reserve home with you from the visitor center shop. Discover books on Icelandic flora and fauna, handcrafted reindeer antler souvenirs, and locally produced jams and chutneys, all sourced from the surrounding wilderness.
- **Vigur Island Puffin Shop:** If you're lucky enough to visit Vigur Island, take advantage of the Puffin Shop, a haven for puffin-themed souvenirs. Pick up adorable puffin plushies, quirky puffin magnets, and even puffin-shaped chocolates, guaranteed to bring a smile to your face.

Did You Know: The Westfjords Heritage Museum houses over 17,000 artifacts, offering a glimpse into the region's fascinating past.

Sports and Leisure:
- **Westfjords Ski Touring:** Embrace the winter wonderland of the Westfjords on a ski touring adventure. Glide across pristine snow-covered landscapes, witness frozen waterfalls and towering peaks, and experience the unique thrill of backcountry skiing in this remote paradise.
- **Westfjords Fishing:** Cast your line in the pristine waters of the Westfjords, a haven for anglers of all levels. Reel in cod, haddock, and even halibut, or try your luck fly-fishing for Arctic char in pristine rivers and lakes. Immerse yourself in the local fishing culture and savor the freshest seafood you'll ever taste.
- **Westfjords Birdwatching:** The Westfjords offer a birdwatcher's paradise, with diverse species like puffins, guillemots, and Arctic terns calling the region home. Explore Látrabjarg cliffs, boat around islands brimming with bird life, or wander hidden valleys searching for rare, feathered treasures.
- **Valagil Ravine:** Hike through the stunning Valagil Ravine, a hidden gem offering dramatic beauty and geological wonders. Witness towering basalt columns rising from the ravine floor, explore hidden waterfalls tucked away in the cliffs, and feel the power of nature's sculpting forces.

Accommodations:
- **Ísafjörður Bed and Breakfast:** Experience Icelandic hospitality at a charming bed and breakfast in Ísafjörður. Enjoy cozy rooms,

delicious homemade breakfasts, and insider tips on exploring the town and surrounding regions.
- **Vatnsfjörður Cottages:** Immerse yourself in the tranquility of the Vatnsfjörður Nature Reserve with a stay in a traditional turf cottage. Experience the unique atmosphere of these historical dwellings, wake up to breathtaking mountain views, and enjoy the peace of the Icelandic countryside.
- **Westfjords Adventure in Patreksfjörður:** Embrace the spirit of adventure at Westfjords Adventures, offering a unique glamping experience. Stay in comfortable dome tents with panoramic views, participate in guided hikes and kayaking tours, and gather around cozy campfires under the endless summer sky.
- **Malarhorn Guesthouse:** Enjoy the warmth of Icelandic hospitality at the Malarhorn Guesthouse, offering comfortable rooms and stunning fjord views. Savor home-cooked meals prepared with local ingredients, relax in the communal living area, and share stories with fellow travelers who have fallen under the Westfjords' spell.

Westfjords Unbound: Unveiling Hidden Gems and Practical Tips

The Westfjords whisper secrets beyond the usual tourist trail. Here are some hidden gems and practical tips to enrich your experience in each aspect:

Hidden Gems:
- **Ísafjörður:** Beyond the vibrant harbor, explore the hidden artwork scattered around town. Look for the "Sea Troll" sculpture near the harbor, the "Whale Bone Arch" in the Westfjords Heritage Museum garden, and the whimsical "Birdhouses of Ísafjörður" tucked away in unexpected corners.
- **Drangsnes:** Hike to the abandoned village of Hesteyri, accessible only by foot or boat. Witness remnants of a bygone era and imagine the lives of the fishermen who once called this place home.

Drangsnes.
Bromr at Dutch Wikipedia, CC BY-SA 3.0 <https://creativecommons.org/licenses/by-sa/3.0>, via Wikimedia Commons: https://commons.wikimedia.org/wiki/File:Kerling-Drangsnes.JPG

- **Hornstrandir:** Explore the secluded bay of Hvitanes, reachable by a challenging but rewarding hike. Discover hidden hot springs, soak in the untouched beauty of the landscape, and feel the weight of history in the abandoned shepherd's hut.

- **Látrabjarg:** Explore the southern part of the cliffs, less crowded than the main viewpoint, for a more peaceful encounter with the bird life and dramatic coastline.

- **Vatnsfjörður Nature Reserve:** Visit the abandoned farmhouse of Hrafnseyri, now a museum with exhibits showing the lives of farmers in the region. Explore the surrounding natural wonders, from hidden waterfalls to ancient burial mounds.

Vatnsfjörður Nature Reserve.
Berserkur, CC BY-SA 4.0 <https://creativecommons.org/licenses/by-sa/4.0>, via Wikimedia Commons: https://commons.wikimedia.org/wiki/File:Vatnsfj%C3%B6r%C3%B0ur,_BS.jpg

- **Rauðasandur (Red Sand Beach):** Hike to the nearby hot springs for a relaxing dip in geothermal waters after enjoying the unique red sand beach.

Rauðasandur.

Evgeniy Metyolkin, CC BY-SA 3.0 <https://creativecommons.org/licenses/by-sa/3.0>, via Wikimedia Commons: https://commons.wikimedia.org/wiki/File:Rau%C3%B0asandur,_longest_beach_in_WestFjords_-_panoramio.jpg

- **Vigur Island:** Take a boat tour to explore the island's hidden coves and rocky shores, teeming with puffins and other seabirds.

Vigur Island.
Christian Bickel fingalo, CC BY-SA 4.0 <https://creativecommons.org/licenses/by-sa/4.0>, via Wikimedia Commons: https://commons.wikimedia.org/wiki/File:Island_Vigur.jpg

Practical Tips:

- **Weather:** Pack layers, waterproof gear, and sturdy shoes for all weather conditions. The Westfjords can experience sudden changes in weather, so be prepared for anything.
- **Transportation:** Consider renting a car for maximum flexibility, but be aware of the narrow roads and challenging driving conditions in some areas. Public buses and organized tours are available for those who prefer not to drive.
- **Accommodation:** Book your accommodation well in advance, especially during peak season, as options are limited in some areas.
- **Supplies:** Stock up on groceries and essentials in larger towns like Ísafjörður and Húsavík before venturing into remote areas.
- **Respect the Environment:** Leave no trace behind, respect wildlife, and follow local regulations to preserve the fragile ecosystem of the Westfjords.

- **Embrace the Slower Pace:** Disconnect from technology, slow down, and savor the tranquility of the Westfjords. Enjoy the silence, the stunning scenery, and the unique atmosphere of this remote region.

By venturing beyond the usual tourist trail and embracing these hidden gems and practical tips, you'll unlock a deeper understanding of the Westfjords and create memories that will last a lifetime.

As the sun dips below the horizon, casting long shadows on the fjord waters, it's time to bid farewell to the wild magic of the Westfjords. But fear not, its memories will linger like the mist clinging to the mountains, echoing in the cries of seabirds and the stories whispered by the wind. You'll leave this remote paradise with hearts full of wonder, senses awakened by the raw beauty, and souls etched with the spirit of adventure.

The Westfjords are more than just a destination; they are an experience, a whisper of what Iceland once was . . . an invitation to lose yourself in the embrace of nature. So, go forth, dear traveler, and carry the magic of the Westfjords with you, a reminder that the truly breathtaking lies not in crowded streets but in the untamed corners of the world.

Chapter 7: North Iceland

Forget sun-drenched beaches and bustling nightlife. In North Iceland, ruggedness reigns supreme, painting landscapes with strokes of moss green, obsidian black, and glacier sapphire. This remote tapestry, woven from volcanic plains, jagged peaks, and shimmering fjords, beckons hikers, adventure seekers, and those yearning to escape the city buzz. Here, where the Arctic wind whispers tales of Viking sagas and the midnight sun casts an ethereal glow, prepare to embrace the rawness of nature and embark on a journey through landscapes like no other.

From gentle walks weaving through geothermal wonderlands to challenging climbs scaling snow-capped giants, North Iceland offers a playground for every adventurer's spirit. Lace up your boots, silence your phone, and let the whispers of the north guide you as you discover the untamed charm and endless possibilities that lie within this breathtaking corner of the world.

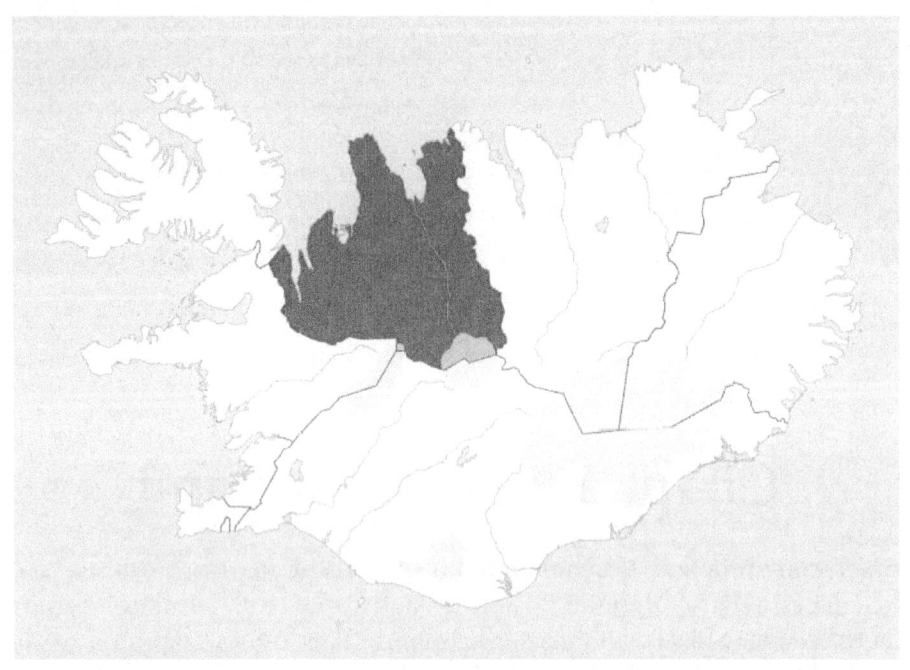

North Iceland.
Karte: NordNordWest, Lizenz: Creative Commons by-sa-3.0 de, CC BY-SA 3.0 DE <https://creativecommons.org/licenses/by-sa/3.0/de/deed.en>, via Wikimedia Commons. https://commons.wikimedia.org/wiki/File:Nor%C3%B0urland_vestra_in_Iceland_2018.svg

Northeast Iceland: Where Fire and Ice Dance in a Symphony of Wonder

Beyond the glaciers' icy grip and volcanic vents' fiery breath lies Northeast Iceland, a land where nature sculpts landscapes with brutal beauty and the whispers of Viking sagas cling to the wind. Here, where geothermal springs paint the earth in vibrant colors and waterfalls thunder like ancient hymns, awaits a tapestry of adventure woven from volcanic majesty, serene lakes, and the raw wilderness of the Arctic North.

Historical Background:

Etched in this region's rugged terrain are whispers of Viking sagas, tales of brave explorers and mythical creatures. Norse settlers carved a life from the volcanic plains, leaving behind remnants of longhouses and burial mounds that stand as silent testaments to their resilience. Centuries later, geothermal energy fueled the growth of towns like Akureyri, transforming them into vibrant cultural hubs nestled amid breathtaking landscapes.

Main Attractions:
- **Akureyri:** As the "Capital of North Iceland," Akureyri offers a charming blend of urban delights and natural wonders. Explore the lively harbor, browse vibrant shops, delve into history at the Akureyri Art Museum, or ascend Mt. Hlíðarfjall for breathtaking ski slopes and panoramic views.

Akureyri.
Virtual-Pano, CC BY-SA 4.0 <https://creativecommons.org/licenses/by-sa/4.0>, via Wikimedia Commons: https://commons.wikimedia.org/wiki/File:03613_ISL_Akureyri_cruise_vessel_vapors_V_P.jpg

- **Húsavík:** Calling all whale enthusiasts! Húsavík, the "Whale-Watching Capital of Europe," offers the thrill of sailing alongside majestic humpback whales, playful minke whales, and pods of dolphins. Learn about these gentle giants at the Húsavík Whale Museum, and let the whispers of the ocean fill your soul.

As of the writing of this book, the normal opening hours for the Husavik Whale Museum are 9 AM to 6 PM every day. Please double-check the opening hours online should there have been any slight change in their schedule.

Húsavík.
Eysteinn Guðni Guðnason, CC BY-SA 4.0 <https://creativecommons.org/licenses/by-sa/4.0>, via Wikimedia Commons:
https://commons.wikimedia.org/wiki/File:H%C3%BAsav%C3%ADk_2023_aerial.jpg

- **Lake Mývatn:** Immerse yourself in a geothermal wonderland at Lake Mývatn. Hike. In the midst of lava fields and pseudo-craters, witness vibrant bird life at the Sigurgeir's Bird Museum or soak in the milky blue waters of the Mývatn Nature Baths.

Lake Mývatn.
Spike, CC BY-SA 4.0 <https://creativecommons.org/licenses/by-sa/4.0>, via Wikimedia Commons:
https://commons.wikimedia.org/wiki/File:M%C3%BDvatn_Dimmuborgir_Panorama_01.jpg

- **Dettifoss Waterfall:** Prepare to be awestruck by Dettifoss, the second most powerful waterfall in Europe. Feel the earth tremble beneath your feet as the thunderous cascade plunges 44 meters into the Jökulsá canyon, a spectacle of raw power and natural beauty.

Dettifoss Waterfall.
Spike, CC BY-SA 4.0 <https://creativecommons.org/licenses/by-sa/4.0>, via Wikimedia Commons: https://commons.wikimedia.org/wiki/File:Dettifoss_Panorama_03.jpg

- **Dimmuborgir (The Dark Castles):** Enter a realm of volcanic lore at Dimmuborgir. Explore lava formations resembling black castles and caves said to be inhabited by hidden trolls. Let your imagination run wild in this otherworldly landscape.

Dimmuborgir.
*Tord Dellsen, CC0, via Wikimedia Commons:
https://commons.wikimedia.org/wiki/File:Dimmuborgir_lava_structure.jpg*

- **Goðafoss (Waterfall of the Gods):** Witness the cascading beauty of Goðafoss, where legend tells of pagan idols being cast into the waters during Iceland's conversion to Christianity. Hike behind the falls for a unique perspective or marvel at its majesty from the viewing platform.

Goðafoss.
Superbass, CC BY-SA 3.0 <*https://creativecommons.org/licenses/by-sa/3.0*>, via Wikimedia Commons:
https://commons.wikimedia.org/wiki/File:Go%C3%B0afoss_Island.jpg

- **Ásbyrgi Canyon:** Hike through the dramatic depths of Ásbyrgi Canyon, carved by ancient glaciers. Follow the tranquil Jökulsá river, ascend Hólmaslétta cliffs for bird's-eye views, or explore hidden waterfalls tucked away within the canyon walls.

Ásbyrgi Canyon.
Michal Klajban, CC BY-SA 4.0 <https://creativecommons.org/licenses/by-sa/4.0>, via Wikimedia Commons: https://commons.wikimedia.org/wiki/File:Canyon,_Hiking_trail_from_Dettifoss_to_%C3%81sbyrgi,_Iceland_1 4.jpg

Experiences:
- **Midnight Sun Hikes:** During the summer months, hike under the ethereal glow of the midnight sun, experiencing landscapes bathed in golden twilight. Witness the play of light and shadow on waterfalls and volcanic peaks, creating a surreal and unforgettable experience.
- **Northern Lights Photography Tours:** In winter, chase the dancing aurora borealis across the dark Icelandic skies. Capture the mesmerizing spectacle of emerald, violet, and turquoise ribbons swirling across the night sky, creating a celestial show like no other.
- **Geothermal Bathing Adventure:** Immerse yourself in the milky blue waters of natural hot springs like the Mývatn Nature Baths or Hverir. Let the soothing geothermal waters replenish your

spirit and soak in the tranquility of the surrounding landscapes.
- **Glacier Ice Cave Exploration:** Embark on a thrilling adventure into the icy heart of an active glacier. Explore hidden caverns, marvel at the intricate ice formations, and witness the raw power of these frozen giants from within.
- **Horseback Riding Through Lava Fields:** Saddle up and explore the unique landscapes of Northeast Iceland on horseback. Traverse black sand deserts, climb volcanic cones, and feel the thrill of riding through this rugged terrain.
- **Traditional Icelandic Food Tour:** Sample the culinary delights of Northeast Iceland, from fresh seafood caught in the North Atlantic to smoked lamb and locally made cheeses. Discover hidden cafes and charming restaurants and let your taste buds experience the region's unique flavors.

Did You Know: The Sigurgeir's Bird Museum boasts the largest private bird collection in Iceland, with over 3000 specimens.

Family Fun:
- **Whale-Watching Tours:** Spark a sense of wonder in your children with a thrilling whale-watching adventure. Watch with delight as humpback whales breach and dolphins frolic alongside the boat, creating memories that will last a lifetime.
- **Akureyri Children's Pool:** Let your little ones splash and play in the heated seawater pool at Akureyri swimming pool. Enjoy waterslides, climbing structures, and a café while overlooking the picturesque fjord.
- **Mývatn Nature Baths:** Family fun awaits at the Mývatn Nature Baths. Soak in the geothermal waters, explore the surrounding lava fields, and build sandcastles on the black sand beach. This unique hot spring experience is perfect for families of all ages.

Where to Eat:
- **Skálinn Restaurant (Akureyri):** Sample modern Icelandic cuisine with breathtaking fjord views at Skálinn Restaurant. Savor fresh seafood, locally sourced lamb dishes, and creative vegetarian options, all prepared with seasonal ingredients.
- **Gamla Bakaríið (Húsavík):** Experience the charm of a traditional Icelandic bakery at Gamla Bakaríið. Indulge in freshly baked pastries, hearty sandwiches, and homemade soups, all made with

local ingredients and love.

- **Vogajos Restaurant (Lake Mývatn):** Enjoy panoramic views of Lake Mývatn while savoring delicious Icelandic fare at Vogafjos Restaurant. Try the smoked trout, reindeer carpaccio, or the traditional lamb soup, all served with warm Icelandic hospitality.

Did You Know: The name Ásbyrgi Canyon translates to "Shelter of the Gods," a legend telling of the god Thor dragging his giant chariot through the earth, creating the dramatic natural formation.

Shopping Guide:

- **Akureyri Art Museum Shop:** Find unique Icelandic souvenirs and handcrafted treasures at the Akureyri Art Museum Shop. Browse handcrafted jewelry, woolen sweaters, and artwork inspired by the region's stunning landscapes.
- **Myvatn Nature Baths Shop:** Pamper yourself or find the perfect gift at the Myvatn Nature Baths shop. Indulge in Icelandic skincare products, pick up volcanic souvenirs, or choose from a selection of cozy Icelandic sweaters.
- **Húsavík Whale Watching Center Shop:** Take a piece of whale watching magic home with you from the Húsavík Whale Watching Centre shop. Discover educational toys, plush whale souvenirs, and handcrafted jewelry depicting these gentle giants.

Sports and Leisure:

- **Mountaineering:** Challenge yourself on the snow-capped peaks of Northeast Iceland. Ascend Hvannadalshnjúkur, Iceland's highest peak, or conquer the Vatnajökull glacier for breathtaking views and unforgettable experiences.
- **Whitewater Rafting:** Thrill seekers, rejoice! Navigate the surging rapids of glacial rivers like Jökulsá or Þjórsá on a whitewater rafting adventure. Feel the adrenaline rush as you navigate the unpredictable waters and witness the dramatic landscapes from a unique perspective.
- **Fly Fishing:** Cast your line in the pristine waters of Northeast Iceland and discover a fisherman's paradise. Reel in Arctic char, trout, and even Atlantic salmon from serene lakes and hidden rivers.
- **Birdwatching:** With diverse habitats and over 300 bird species, Northeast Iceland is a haven for birdwatchers. Spot iconic puffins

at Langanes peninsula, observe majestic gyrfalcons soaring above Lake Mývatn, or listen to the haunting calls of Arctic terns nesting along the coast.

Did You Know: The Hverir hot springs are home to the "Boiling Mud Pots," bubbling cauldrons of mud and sulfuric gases that paint a surreal picture of geothermal activity.

Accommodations:

- **Akureyri Backpackers:** Budget-conscious travelers will find comfort and camaraderie at the Akureyri Backpackers hostel. Enjoy a lively atmosphere, shared kitchen facilities, and a convenient location close to all the city's attractions.
- **Mývatn Natura Apartments:** Immerse yourself in the serenity of Lake Mývatn with a stay at the Mývatn Natura Apartments. Enjoy cozy cabins with modern amenities, breathtaking lake views, and easy access to geothermal baths and nature trails.
- **Krafla Geothermal Hotel:** Experience the unique luxury of a geothermal hotel at Krafla. Sink into hot springs while gazing at volcanic landscapes, indulge in spa treatments, and savor delicious meals in the geothermal restaurant.

Transportation:

Flying into Akureyri Airport is the quickest option, offering panoramic views of the region upon arrival. Public buses connect Akureyri with other towns in the area, but renting a car provides greater flexibility for exploring hidden gems and remote corners. Ferry services are available for those arriving from mainland Iceland.

Don't Miss:

- **Trollaskagi Peninsula:** Venture off the beaten path to the Trollaskagi Peninsula, a hidden gem in Northeast Iceland. Hike through rugged mountains, ski pristine slopes, and spot elusive Arctic foxes in this untouched wilderness.
- **Heimskautsgerðið, the Arctic Henge:** Discover Iceland's answer to Stonehenge at Heimskautsgerðið, a mysterious stone circle dating back to the Viking era. Explore the theories surrounding its purpose, marvel at its ancient presence, and let your imagination wander in the stark beauty of the landscape.
- **Krafla Caldera and Viti Crater:** Witness the raw power of geothermal activity at Krafla Caldera. Hike to the Viti crater, a

vibrant turquoise lake formed by a volcanic eruption, and feel the earth's heat radiating from the surrounding vents and fumaroles.
- **Hverir Hot Springs:** Immerse yourself in the otherworldly beauty of the Hverir hot springs. Walk amongst bubbling mud pots, hissing steam vents, and colorful sulfur deposits, feeling like you've stepped onto another planet.

Remember:
- Northeast Iceland's weather can be unpredictable, so pack layers and waterproof gear for all seasons.
- Respect the fragile ecosystems and local customs. Leave no trace and be mindful of your impact on this unique environment.
- Embrace the slower pace of life and disconnect from technology. Let the silence and beauty of the landscapes wash over you.
- Be prepared for limited services and longer travel times in remote areas. Download offline maps and plan accordingly.

Northeast Iceland is not just a destination. It's an invitation to reconnect with nature's raw power, discover hidden gems, and create memories that will last a lifetime. As you step off the airport, prepare to be captivated by the symphony of fire and ice that dances in this unforgettable corner of the world.

Northwest Iceland: Where Rugged Wilderness Meets Viking Whispers

Beyond the Arctic Circle's icy grip, beneath the watchful gaze of snow-capped peaks, lies Northwest Iceland. This land, sculpted by ancient glaciers and volcanic fires, beckons adventurers with untamed beauty and endless possibilities. Here, seals bask on black sand beaches, and waterfalls thunder through moss-carpeted valleys. It's a tapestry of experiences woven from glacial wonder, remote villages, and the raw wilderness of the North Atlantic.

Historical Background:

Northwest Iceland's rugged terrain bears the footprints of Viking settlers who sailed across treacherous seas, carving a life from the barren shores. Þingeyrarkirkja, one of the oldest stone churches in Iceland, dating back to the 19th century, is a testament to their resilience and faith. Sagas of daring heroes and mythical creatures echo within the windswept landscapes, whispering tales of ancient battles and hidden treasures.

Main Attractions:

- **Skagafjörður:** This scenic fjord, nestled amongst towering mountains, beckons adventure seekers. Raft the glacial waters of the Austari Jökulsá River, kayak amidst icebergs, or hike through untouched valleys, each step revealing breathtaking panoramas.

Skagafjörður.
Hornstrandir1, CC BY-SA 4.0 <https://creativecommons.org/licenses/by-sa/4.0>, via Wikimedia Commons: https://commons.wikimedia.org/wiki/File:Skagafj%C3%B6r%C3%B0ur_mountain.jpg

- **Hvítserkur:** Witness the dramatic silhouette of Hvítserkur, where wind and waves have sculpted the volcanic rock into an iconic troll-like figure. Let your imagination wander among the legends surrounding this natural wonder.

Hvítserkur.
Alexander Grebenkov, CC BY 3.0 <https://creativecommons.org/licenses/by/3.0>, via Wikimedia Commons: https://commons.wikimedia.org/wiki/File:Hv%C3%ADtserkur_in_July,_2019.jpg

- **Kálfshamarsvík:** Embrace the raw beauty of the North Atlantic at Kálfshamarsvík. Explore dramatic cliffs, discover hidden coves, and stand awestruck before the majestic rock formations sculpted by wind and sea.

Kálfshamarsvík.
Zoran Kurelić Rabko, CC BY-SA 3.0 <https://creativecommons.org/licenses/by-sa/3.0>, via Wikimedia Commons: https://commons.wikimedia.org/wiki/File:Kalfhamarsvik,_Iceland_-_panoramio.jpg

- **Drangey Island:** Steeped in Viking lore, Drangey Island beckons with its dramatic cliffs and hidden caves. Hike to the island's peak for panoramic views, listen to tales of trolls and hidden treasures, and feel the weight of history within its ancient ruins.

Drangey Island.
Bromr, CC BY-SA 3.0 <https://creativecommons.org/licenses/by-sa/3.0>, via Wikimedia Commons: https://commons.wikimedia.org/wiki/File:Drangey2010.JPG

Transport:

Reaching Northwest Iceland is part of the adventure. Fly into Akureyri Airport and continue your journey by car, enjoying the scenic landscapes along the way. Public buses connect some towns, but renting a car provides greater flexibility for exploring hidden gems. Ferries from mainland Iceland offer an alternative mode of transportation.

Did You Know: Grímsey Island, nestled on the Arctic Circle, holds the unique title of Iceland's northernmost inhabited point. During summer, experience the magic of the midnight sun, where daylight casts an ethereal glow for 24 hours straight.

Experiences:
- **Glacier Exploration Tours**: Embark on a thrilling adventure onto the Langjökull glacier, exploring hidden ice caves, crevasses, and glacial mills. Feel the power of ancient ice beneath your feet and witness the mesmerizing beauty of this frozen wonderland.
- **Whale Watching Adventures**: Sail beneath the Arctic sky and witness the majesty of humpback whales, playful dolphins, and minke whales breaching in the frigid waters. Listen to their haunting songs, learn about their conservation, and create memories that will last a lifetime.
- **Viking Saga Trails**: Hike through landscapes once tread upon by Viking heroes, guided by local storytellers who bring their sagas to life. Trace the footsteps of explorers, unravel ancient mysteries, and connect with the region's rich cultural heritage.
- **Geothermal Soaking Under the Midnight Sun**: Immerse yourself in the soothing waters of hidden geothermal pools as the midnight sun paints the sky in an ethereal glow. Experience the serenity of being enveloped by nature's warmth under the endless light of the summer Arctic night.
- **Arctic Circle Celebration**: Join the vibrant festivities on Grímsey Island during the summer solstice. Celebrate the unique magic of being directly on the Arctic Circle, participate in traditional Icelandic dances, sample local delicacies, and experience the warmth of island life under the never-setting sun.

Family Fun:
- **Húsafell Nature Park**: This family-friendly park offers a playground, swimming pool, and diverse outdoor activities like horseback riding, glacier jeeps, and hiking trails suitable for all ages. Explore waterfalls, lava caves, and hidden coves, creating lasting memories for the whole family.
- **Seal-Watching Tours**: Witness the playful antics of harbor seals on boat tours along the dramatic coastline. See these adorable creatures basking on black sand beaches, swimming alongside the boat, and delight your children with their curious nature.
- **Þingeyrarkirkja Church**: Step back in time and explore the historic Þingeyrarkirkja church with its unique architecture. Children will love the intriguing stories surrounding its

construction and the graveyard with moss-covered headstones.
- **The Troll of Hvítserkur:** Let your imagination run wild at the iconic Hvítserkur rock formation. Tell your children stories of the troll guarding the Vatnsnes peninsula and watch their faces light up with wonder as they explore the surrounding volcanic landscape.
- **Grímsey Island Adventure:** Experience the unique island life of Grímsey with your family. Build sandcastles on black sand beaches, explore the charming church, and let your children run free in the open Arctic air.

Did You Know: Hvítserkur, the iconic rock formation resembling a troll guarding the Vatnsnes peninsula, inspired generations of artists and storytellers, sparking whispers of its supernatural origins.

Where to Eat:
- **Naustið Bistro (Húsavík):** Savor the freshest seafood at Naustið Bistro, overlooking Húsavík Harbor. Enjoy panoramic views while indulging in locally caught fish, gourmet burgers, and inventive vegetarian options.
- **Bjarg Restaurant (Skagafjörður):** Experience contemporary Icelandic cuisine with breathtaking fjord views at Bjarg Restaurant. Sample lamb dishes flavored with wild herbs, locally sourced vegetables, and creative desserts, all in a stylish setting.
- **Lækjarbrekka (Þingeyrarkirkja):** Savor homemade Icelandic fare at Lækjarbrekka, housed in a charming farmhouse near the historic church. Enjoy traditional lamb soup, fresh pastries, and locally made jams in a warm and welcoming atmosphere.
- **Hraun Bistro (Vatnsnes):** Indulge in delicious comfort food at Hraun Bistro, nestled amidst the volcanic landscapes of Vatnsnes. Warm up with hearty soups, homemade stews, and Icelandic pancakes, all made with fresh local ingredients.
- **Grímsey Island Guesthouse:** Experience authentic island life and enjoy fresh seafood dishes at the Grímsey Island Guesthouse. Sample the catch of the day, homemade bread, and traditional Icelandic desserts, all prepared with the island's unique flavor.

Shopping Guide:
- **Húsavík Whale Museum Shop:** Find the perfect whale-themed souvenir at the Húsavík Whale Museum shop. Browse

handcrafted jewelry, plush whales, and educational toys, all supporting conservation efforts.
- **Skagafjörður Folk Museum Shop:** Discover hidden treasures at the Skagafjörður Folk Museum shop. Explore locally made woolen sweaters, traditional Icelandic crafts, and unique souvenirs inspired by the region's rich cultural heritage.
- **Þingeyrarkirkja Church Shop:** Take home a piece of history from the Þingeyrarkirkja Church shop. Find handmade religious figures, local honey, and Icelandic treats, all while supporting the church's preservation efforts.
- **Hand Gjörð í Búðum (Vatnsnes):** Immerse yourself in the world of Icelandic artisans at Hand Gjörð í Búðum, a cooperative shop selling locally crafted jewelry, pottery, and textile art. Find unique souvenirs and gifts celebrating the region's creativity.
- **Grímsey Island Craft Shop:** Support local artists and find one-of-a-kind souvenirs at the Grímsey Island Craft Shop. Browse hand-knitted woolen hats, locally painted postcards, and unique trinkets crafted with island life in mind.

Did You Know: Northwest Iceland boasts some of the country's most remote geothermal pools, hidden in volcanic landscapes and offering a chance to soak in the natural warmth in complete solitude.

Entertainment:
- **Akureyri Arts Festival (June/July):** Immerse yourself in the vibrant arts scene at the Akureyri Arts Festival, held annually in June and July. Enjoy theater performances, live music, art exhibitions, and street performers, all within the charming surroundings of Akureyri.
- **Secret Lagoon Open Air Cinema (Summer):** Enjoy a unique movie experience under the midnight sun at the Secret Lagoon Open Air Cinema. Relax in the geothermal waters of the Secret Lagoon while watching classic films projected onto a screen with the dramatic Icelandic landscape as a backdrop.
- **Galdramál: Viking Village Festival (July):** Travel back in time at the Galdramál: Viking Village Festival held in July. Witness historical reenactments, participate in traditional crafts workshops, enjoy Viking feasts, and let the drumbeat of their music transport you to the era of sagas and warriors.

- **The Northern Lights (Winter):** Chase the dancing aurora borealis across the inky skies during the winter months. Embark on guided tours, find secluded viewing spots away from light pollution, and witness the celestial spectacle of emerald, violet, and turquoise ribbons swirling across the Arctic night.

Sports and Leisure:
- **Hiking and Mountaineering:** Conquer the rugged peaks of Northwest Iceland, from the glaciers of Langjökull to the volcanic slopes of Snæfellsnes. Challenge yourself on diverse trails, witness breathtaking panoramas, and experience the exhilarating feeling of reaching the summit.
- **Whitewater Rafting:** Navigate the churning rapids of glacial rivers like Jökulsá or Þjórsá in an adrenaline-pumping whitewater rafting adventure. Feel the power of the rushing water, navigate wild currents, and experience the thrill of conquering the rapids as a team.
- **Sea Kayaking:** Explore hidden coves and secluded beaches from a unique perspective on a sea kayaking adventure. Paddle alongside playful seals, witness the dramatic cliffs from the water's edge, and let the rhythmic sound of the waves lull you into serenity.
- **Birdwatching:** Northwest Iceland is a haven for birdwatchers, with diverse habitats attracting over 300 bird species. Observe puffins nesting on cliffs, listen to the haunting calls of Arctic terns, and spot elusive gyrfalcons soaring above the mountains.
- **Horseback Riding:** Embark on a traditional Icelandic horseback riding experience, traversing black sand beaches, volcanic plains, and hidden valleys. Connect with these unique Icelandic horses, known for their five gaits, and let them carry you through the breathtaking landscapes of this remote region.

Accommodations:
- **Húsafell Guesthouse:** Enjoy comfort and convenience at the Húsafell Guesthouse, a perfect base for exploring the surrounding glacial wonders. Choose from cozy rooms, cabins, or camping facilities, and enjoy the guesthouse's welcoming atmosphere and helpful staff.

- **Skagafjörður Camping and Cottages:** Immerse yourself in the pristine nature of Skagafjörður at the Camping and Cottages. Pitch your tent amidst stunning vistas, rent a cozy cabin for added comfort, or enjoy the communal barbecue area and shared facilities.
- **Hellnafell Guesthouse:** Experience historic charm at the Hellnafell Guesthouse, located near the iconic church. Stay in the renovated parsonage or choose from comfortable modern rooms, all offering a unique glimpse into Iceland's past.
- **Vatnsnes Farm Holidays:** Embrace the idyllic countryside at a Vatnsnes farm holiday. Stay in a traditional Icelandic farmhouse, enjoy farm-fresh meals, and participate in daily activities like sheep herding or horseback riding.
- **Grímsey Island Guesthouse:** Experience the simplicity of island life at the Grímsey Island Guesthouse. Stay in comfortable guest rooms, enjoy fresh seafood meals, and immerse yourself in the close-knit community of this unique Arctic outpost.

Remember:
- Respect the fragile ecosystems and local customs. Leave no trace and be mindful of your impact on this pristine environment.
- Embrace the slower pace of life and disconnect from technology. Let the silence and beauty of the landscapes wash over you.
- Be prepared for limited services and longer travel times in remote areas.

As the northern lights dance across the night sky, painting the mountains with celestial brushstrokes, it's time to bid farewell to the untamed magic of North Iceland. Yet, fear not, for its memories will linger like the mist clinging to volcanic peaks, echoing in the cries of seabirds and the stories whispered by the wind. You will leave this remote paradise with a heart full of wonder, eyes brimming with landscapes etched in memory, and your soul rejuvenated by the raw beauty of nature.

Go forth, dear traveler, and carry the whisper of the north with you, a reminder that true beauty lies not in crowded cityscapes but in the unbridled heart of nature. And perhaps, on your way out, take a detour along the Diamond Circle, a legendary route linking together breathtaking natural wonders like Dettifoss, the most powerful waterfall in Europe, and the majestic Ásbyrgi canyon carved by ancient glaciers; for in North Iceland, every journey unveils a new diamond waiting to be discovered.

Chapter 8: East Iceland

Beyond the icy grip of glaciers and the watchful gaze of volcanic peaks lies East Iceland. A land where ancient sagas whisper on the wind and rugged landscapes paint a breathtaking tapestry of fire and ice. This region, known as *Austurland*, beckons with its diverse beauty, welcoming travelers with fjord-side villages, towering waterfalls, and vibrant cultural experiences. From charming towns brimming with art and music festivals to the desolate grandeur of Vatnajökull National Park, East Iceland offers something for every adventurer, artist, and soul seeking solace in nature's symphony.

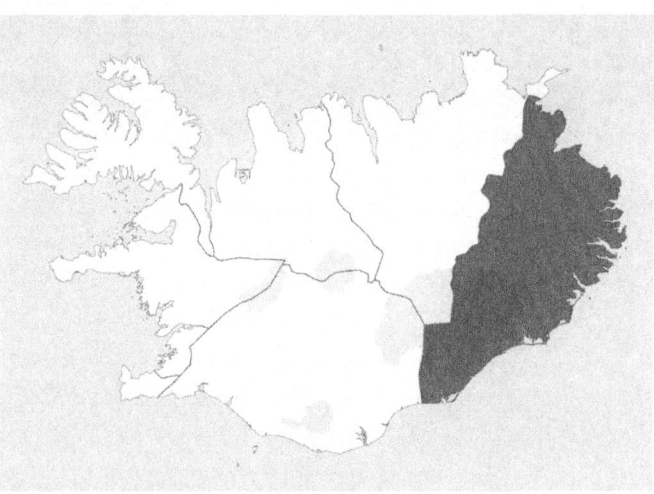

East Iceland.
TUBS, CC BY-SA 3.0 <https://creativecommons.org/licenses/by-sa/3.0>, via Wikimedia Commons. https://commons.wikimedia.org/wiki/File:Austurland_in_Iceland.svg

Historical Background

East Iceland's history stretches back to the days of Viking settlers who braved the treacherous North Atlantic to carve a life from this untamed land. Sagas speak of fierce warriors, mystical creatures, and hidden treasures waiting to be discovered. Centuries later, the region flourished as a center of trade and culture, leaving behind a legacy of charming towns, quaint museums, and captivating folklore. Today, East Iceland preserves its unique heritage while embracing a vibrant contemporary spirit, inviting you to step into a world where past and present intertwine.

Main Attractions

- **Egilsstaðir:** The "Capital of East Iceland," Egilsstaðir offers a charming blend of urban delights and natural wonders. Explore the vibrant art scene, delve into local history at the East Iceland Heritage Museum, or hike to the scenic Hengifoss and Fardagafoss waterfalls.

Egilsstaðir.
Eysteinn Guðni Guðnason, CC BY-SA 4.0 <https://creativecommons.org/licenses/by-sa/4.0>, via Wikimedia Commons: https://commons.wikimedia.org/wiki/File:Egilssta%C3%B0ir_2023.jpg

- **Seyðisfjörður:** Nestled amongst colorful houses and dram. fjords, Seyðisfjörður is a haven for art lovers and outdo enthusiasts. Immerse yourself in the vibrant arts scene, explo the Seyðisfjörður Fjord on a kayak, or hike to the Svartifos waterfall, its dark basalt columns contrasting with the cascading water.

Seyðisfjörður.

Ira Goldstein, CC BY-SA 3.0 <https://creativecommons.org/licenses/by-sa/3.0>, via Wikimedia Commons: https://commons.wikimedia.org/wiki/File:Sey%C3%B0isfj%C3%B6r%C3%B0ur,_Iceland.jpg

- **Vatnajökull National Park:** This UNESCO World Heritage site encompasses Europe's largest glacier, Vatnajökull, a frozen giant offering breathtaking landscapes and diverse adventures. Hike through volcanic craters, explore hidden ice caves, or embark on a thrilling glacier tour, witnessing the raw power of nature.

As of the writing of this book, the site is open every day, 24 hours a day.

- **The East Fjords:** These ancient fjords, carved by glaciers millennia ago, are a symphony of rugged beauty. Kayak through turquoise waters, hike to hidden waterfalls, or explore charming villages like Stöðvarfjörður, Fáskrúðsfjörður, and Reyðarfjörður, each with its unique character and stories to tell.

The East Fjords.

sergejf, CC BY-SA 2.0 <https://creativecommons.org/licenses/by-sa/2.0>, via Wikimedia Commons: https://commons.wikimedia.org/wiki/File:East_Fjords_(15849632363).jpg

- **Petra's Stone and Mineral Collection:** Discover a hidden gem in Stöðvarfjörður, where Petra displays her incredible collection of minerals and rocks, each with its own captivating story. Learn about the region's geological history and marvel at the dazzling array of colors and textures.

As of the writing of this book, the normal opening hours are every day, from 9 AM to 5 PM, but please double-check the opening hours online should there have been any slight change in their schedule.

- **Lagarfljót River:** Legend tells of a monstrous serpent lurking in the depths of Lagarfljót River. Embark on a monster-hunting cruise, cast your line for Arctic char in the crystal-clear waters, or simply soak in the tranquility of the surrounding landscapes.

Lagarfljót River.
Spike, CC BY-SA 4.0 <https://creativecommons.org/licenses/by-sa/4.0>, via Wikimedia Commons: https://commons.wikimedia.org/wiki/File:Route_917_J%C3%B6kla_Lagarflj%C3%B3t_H%C3%A9ra%C3%B0ssandur_Panorama_01.jpg

Did You Know: East Iceland boasts Europe's largest glacier, Vatnajökull, which covers an astounding 8% of the country's landmass.

Transport

Flying into Egilsstaðir Airport is the most convenient option, offering direct connections from Reykjavík and other major Icelandic hubs. Once here, renting a car provides the flexibility to explore the region's hidden gems and remote corners at your own pace. Public buses connect some towns and villages, but their schedules are limited, especially outside of the summer months.

Experiences

- **Glacier Exploration:** Embark on an unforgettable adventure onto Vatnajökull, exploring hidden ice caves, crevasses, and glacial mills. Witness the raw power of ancient ice, feel the chill of

millennia-old glaciers, and create memories that will last a lifetime.
- **Whale Watching Tours:** Sail the pristine waters of the North Atlantic in search of majestic humpback whales, playful dolphins, and minke whales. Learn about these gentle giants, witness their playful antics, and capture their magic in your photos.
- **Viking Heritage Tours:** Travel back in time with guided tours through the region's Viking settlements, burial mounds, and ancient ruins. Hear stories of legendary heroes, explore archaeological sites, and connect with the region's rich cultural heritage.
- **Art and Music Festivals:** Get lost in the colorful arts scene during East Iceland's summer festivals. Enjoy live music, explore art exhibitions, participate in workshops, and experience the infectious energy of local artists and musicians.
- **Lagarfljót Monster Hunting:** Embark on a lighthearted quest for the mythical Lagarfljót worm. Keep an eye out for ripples on the water's surface, listen to local legends, and join the playful hunt for this elusive creature.

Family Fun
- **Egilsstaðir Swimming Pool:** Enjoy a refreshing dip in the heated pool and water slides at the Egilsstaðir swimming pool. This family-friendly facility offers fun for all ages, from toddlers to teenagers.
- **Horseback Riding Adventures:** Embark on a thrilling horseback riding adventure through the particular landscapes of East Iceland. Choose from gentle family rides to challenging treks and experience the unique connection with these sturdy Icelandic horses.
- **Geocaching Treasure Hunt:** Turn the entire region into a giant treasure hunt with geocaching. Download the app, follow the coordinates, and discover hidden caches while exploring hidden corners of the East Fjords, waterfalls, and even glaciers.
- **Lava Caving Adventures:** Descend to the depths of the earth on a guided lava cave exploration. Marvel at the volcanic formations, learn about the geological wonders of the region, and create an unforgettable family memory in this subterranean world.

- **The East Fjords Fairy Forest:** Discover a fairy tale that comes to life in the East Fjords Fairy Forest. Follow the whimsical path, meet up with quirky sculptures and hidden treasures, and let your inner child's imagination run wild in this enchanted woodland.

Where to Eat

- **Hafdís Pizza (Fáskrúðsfjörður):** Treat your taste buds to delicious wood-fired pizzas at Hafdís Pizza. Choose from classic toppings or opt for adventurous Icelandic lamb and seafood options, all made with fresh local ingredients.
- **The Nailed It Fish & Chip Truck (Höfn):** Grab a quick and delicious bite at the iconic fish and chip truck in Höfn. Savor crispy fries and battered fish, enjoying the casual atmosphere and the breathtaking ocean views.

Did You Know: The region hosts a variety of music and art festivals throughout the summer, transforming sleepy villages into bustling hubs of creativity and celebration.

Shopping Guide

- **Gerðuberg Cultural Center (Egilsstaðir):** Discover unique Icelandic art and crafts at the Gerðuberg Cultural Center. Browse hand-knitted sweaters, locally made jewelry, and pottery created by talented local artists, finding the perfect souvenir or gift.
- **Skaftfell Art Center in Seyðisfjörður:** Support local artists and find one-of-a-kind art pieces at the Skaftfell Art Center shop. Explore paintings, sculptures, and handcrafted items inspired by the region's landscapes and stories.
- **Petra's Stone & Mineral Collection (Stöðvarfjörður):** Unearth treasures at Petra's Stone & Mineral Collection, the world's largest collection of zeolites. Find unique crystals, polished stones, and jewelry crafted from these mesmerizing minerals, a reminder of the region's geological wonders.
- **Hand Gjörð í Búðum (Vatnsnes):** Immerse yourself in the world of Icelandic artisans at Handgjörð í Búðum, a cooperative shop selling locally crafted jewelry, pottery, and textile art. Find unique souvenirs and gifts celebrating the region's creativity.

Entertainment
- **East Iceland Arts Festival:** Witness a vibrant explosion of creativity at the East Iceland Arts Festival held annually in June and July. Enjoy theater performances, live music, art exhibitions, and street performers, all within the charming surroundings of towns across the region.
- **Ljósvöku Nights:** Celebrate the winter solstice against the background of the Ljósvöku Nights festival. Witness the enchanting aurora borealis dancing across the dark skies, participate in traditional bonfires and festivities, and experience the magic of the longest nights.
- **The Secret Lagoon Open Air Cinema:** Enjoy a different movie experience under the midnight sun at the Secret Lagoon Open Air Cinema. Relax in the geothermal waters of the Secret Lagoon while watching classic films projected onto a screen amidst the dramatic Icelandic landscape.
- **The North Iceland Horse Show:** Gaze in wonder at the grace and strength of Icelandic horses at the North Iceland Horse Show. Watch skilled riders demonstrating the five gaits of these unusual horses, participate in workshops, and experience the deep connection between Icelanders and their beloved steeds.

Did You Know: Legend tells of a monstrous worm inhabiting Lagarfljót River, affectionately nicknamed the "Lagarfljót Worm." Keep your eyes peeled for this mythical creature while exploring the area.

Sports and Leisure
- **Hiking and Mountaineering:** Conquer the rugged peaks of East Iceland, traversing the Skaftafell National Park trails, scaling Snæfell mountain, or exploring hidden valleys carved by glaciers. Witness breathtaking panoramas, challenge yourself on various paths, and experience the exhilarating feeling of reaching the summit.
- **Glacial Kayaking:** Paddle among towering icebergs and navigate the pristine waters of Jökulsárlón glacial lagoon on a kayaking adventure. Feel the awe-inspiring presence of glaciers, witness seals basking on ice floes, and experience the serenity of exploring this icy wonderland.

- **Birdwatching:** East Iceland is a haven for birdwatchers, with different habitats attracting over 200 species. Watch majestic white-tailed eagles soaring above the cliffs, listen to the haunting calls of Arctic terns, and spot elusive gyrfalcons perched on mountain peaks.
- **Snorkeling and Diving:** Explore the underwater world of crystal-clear glacial lagoons and geothermal pools. Discover the unexpected treasures of colorful fish, unique marine life, volcanic formations, and the hidden wonders beneath the surface.
- **Horseback Riding Tours:** Take a traditional Icelandic horseback riding tour through mystical landscapes, from geothermal valleys to black sand beaches. Connect with these gentle horses, known for their five gaits, and let them carry you through the breathtaking scenery of this remote region.

Did You Know: East Iceland is home to the world's largest collection of zeolites, a group of minerals with unique properties, at Petra's Stone & Mineral Collection in Stöðvarfjörður.

Accommodations

- **Egilsstaðir Guesthouse:** Enjoy the personal touch and comfort at the Egilsstaðir Guesthouse, a perfect base for exploring the surrounding fjords and mountains. Choose from rooms, apartments, or camping facilities, and enjoy the guesthouse's welcoming atmosphere and helpful staff.
- **Seyðisfjörður Guesthouse:** Immerse yourself in the artistic spirit of Seyðisfjörður at the Guesthouse. Stay in rooms that all overlook the fjord, join art workshops, and enjoy the warm hospitality of this family-run guesthouse.
- **Fosshotel Vatnajökull:** Experience the majesty of Vatnajökull National Park from the doorstep of the Fosshotel Vatnajökull. Relax in comfortable rooms with spectacular glacier views, enjoy delicious meals at the on-site restaurant, and choose from a variety of guided tours and outdoor activities.
- **Petra's Guesthouse (Stöðvarfjörður):** Stay in a traditional Icelandic farmhouse amidst the dramatic East Fjords at Petra's Guesthouse. Discover the region's history and folklore from your friendly hosts, enjoy home-cooked meals, and explore the nearby Petra's Stone & Mineral Collection.

- **Höfn Cottages:** Embrace the local way of life at Höfn Cottages, nestled in the black sand beaches and with ocean views. Rent a cozy cottage equipped with all the necessities, prepare fresh seafood in your kitchenette, and experience the simple pleasures of coastal living.

East Iceland is the jewel nestled in the crown of the land of fire and ice; it beckons with a final flourish. From the glacial whispers of Vatnajökull to the vibrant melody of summer festivals, this region is a symphony of contrasts. Hike through landscapes sculpted by ancient giants, kayak through serene fjords, and lose yourself in the charm of fjord-side villages.

Let the vibrant spirit of East Iceland wash over you, whether you're chasing the elusive Lagarfljót worm, searching for hidden treasures in the East Fjords, or simply soaking in the raw beauty of a land where nature reigns supreme. East Iceland is more than just a destination. It is an experience, a memory etched in the soul, and a reminder that the world's greatest treasures lie in the most unexpected corners.

Chapter 9: Itineraries and Programs

Iceland, the land of fire and ice, beckons with its mesmerizing landscapes, geothermal wonders, and rich cultural tapestry. But crafting the perfect itinerary can feel daunting, especially with such diverse experiences on offer. Fear not, intrepid traveler. This final chapter presents a variety of Iceland itineraries and programs tailored to different travel styles and interests, ensuring you make the most of your precious time in this magical land.

Iceland in 7 Days: The Ring Road Expedition

For those seeking a comprehensive overview of Iceland's iconic sights, the 10-day Ring Road expedition is the ultimate adventure. Buckle up and prepare to traverse volcanoes, glaciers, waterfalls, and charming villages as you circumnavigate the island nation.

CC BY-SA 3.0, https://commons.wikimedia.org/w/index.php?curid=21169

Days One to Two: Reykjavik and the Golden Circle

Immerse yourself in the vibrant capital, Reykjavik. Explore its quirky museums, trendy cafes, and colorful street art. Then, delve into the heart of Iceland's geothermal activity on the Golden Circle route. Witness the Strokkur geyser erupt, peer into the Kerið volcanic crater, and marvel at the cascading Gullfoss waterfall.

Days Three to Four: Northern Delights

Head north to the vibrant city of Akureyri, Iceland's second-largest city. Explore its charming harbor, climb Mt. Hlíðarfjall for stunning views, and soak in the geothermal waters of Mývatn Nature Baths. Explore the otherworldly landscapes of Lake Mývatn, dotted with volcanic craters and steaming geothermal vents.

Days Five to Six: East Fjords and Seyðisfjörður

Venture off the beaten path and explore the rugged beauty of the East Fjords. Hike across dramatic cliffs, discover hidden coves, and soak in the charm of the picturesque village of Seyðisfjörður. Don't miss Petra's Stone & Mineral Collection, which houses the world's largest collection of zeolites.

Day Seven: South Coast Highlights

The South Coast boasts some of Iceland's most dramatic landscapes. Witness the cascading Seljalandsfoss and Skógafoss waterfalls, marvel at the black sand beaches and towering rock formations of Reynisdrangar, and stand in awe of the Sólheimajökull glacier lagoon.

Beyond the Ring Road: Specialized Iceland Programs

While the Ring Road offers a fantastic overview, Iceland has much more to offer. Here are some specialized programs catering to specific interests:

For the Culture Vultures:
- **Viking Sagas and Folklore Tour:** Dive into Iceland's rich history, visiting Viking settlements, ancient burial mounds, and museums.
- **Reykjavik Art and Music Scene:** Immerse yourself in the capital's thriving creative scene, exploring galleries, attending concerts, and meeting local artists.
- **East Iceland Art Festivals:** Participate in the vibrant summer festivals scattered across the East Fjords, enjoying art exhibitions, music, and workshops.

For the Thrill Seekers:
- **Glacier Hiking and Ice Caving:** Explore the otherworldly landscapes of glaciers like Vatnajökull, venturing into ice caves and experiencing the raw power of these frozen giants.
- **Whitewater Rafting and Canyoning:** Navigate the rushing rapids of glacial rivers or drop into hidden canyons, experiencing the adrenaline rush of these adventure activities.
- **Whale Watching Tours:** Sail the North Atlantic in search of majestic humpback whales, playful dolphins, and minke whales.

For the Nature Lovers:
- **Hiking and Camping Adventures:** Immerse yourself in Iceland's breathtaking landscapes, traversing diverse trails, and camping under the midnight sun.
- **Horseback Riding Tours:** Explore the unusual terrain on horseback, connecting with Icelandic horses and experiencing the freedom of the open land.

- **Northern Lights Chase:** Take a trip to a front-row seat to witness the aurora borealis dancing across the dark winter skies, a truly magical experience.

For the Family Fun Seekers:
- **Geothermal Pools and Water Parks:** Enjoy hours of fun at geothermal pools and water parks, perfect for relaxing and refreshing after days of exploring.
- **Whale Watching and Puffin Tours:** Create lasting memories for the whole family as you tour by boat to spot incredible marine life.
- **Lava Caving and Museum Adventures:** Explore hidden lava caves and interactive museums, sparking children's imaginations and keeping them entertained.

Remember:
- Choose the program that best suits your interests and travel style.
- Book accommodation in advance, especially during peak season.
- Respect the fragile ecosystems and local customs. Leave no trace behind except your footprints, and be mindful of your impact on this pristine environment.
- Be prepared for unpredictable weather and pack accordingly. Layers are essential, even in summer.
- Purchase an Iceland Visitor Pass for discounted entry to several popular attractions.
- Embrace the slower pace of life and disconnect from technology. Let the silence and beauty of the landscapes wash over you.

Additional Tips for Specific Programs:
- **For Culture Programs:** Learn a few basic Icelandic phrases to impress the locals and have more fun on your trip. The locals will appreciate your efforts and have a good laugh with you at your pronunciation.
- **For Adventure Programs:** Make sure you are fit enough for these types of excursions, and ensure you have the appropriate gear.
- **For Nature Programs:** Choose the correct footwear for hiking and dress in layers.
- **For Family Programs:** Check age restrictions for activities and plan age-appropriate sightseeing and playtime.

Beyond the Tourist Trail: A Seven-Day Off-the-Beaten-Path Iceland Adventure

Forget the crowds and familiar landmarks. This seven-day itinerary ventures into the untamed corners of Iceland, where hidden gems and raw beauty await the intrepid explorer. Prepare to trade tour buses for rugged hiking trails, bustling Reykjavik for charming fishing villages, and the Golden Circle for geothermal valleys untouched by tourist footprints.

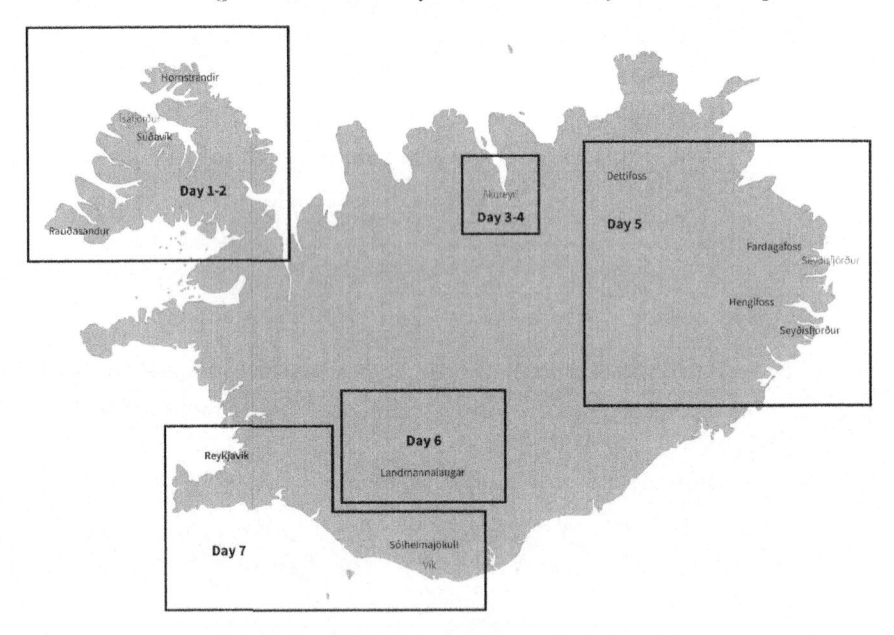

Take a trip through Iceland starting from Akureyri.
OpenStreetMap Contributors: https://www.openstreetmap.org/

Day 1-2: The Westfjords: Where Wild Beauty Reigns

Catch an early ferry to Ísafjörður, the heart of the Westfjords. Rent a car and immerse yourself in this otherworldly landscape of jagged peaks, hidden coves, and crystal-clear fjords. Hike the Hornstrandir nature reserve, spot playful Arctic foxes, and discover remote villages like Súðavík, steeped in local traditions. Don't miss the Rauðasandur red sand beach, a stark contrast against the turquoise waters. Spend the night in a charming guesthouse with ocean views.

Day 3-4: Akureyri – Gateway to the North

Land in Akureyri, Iceland's second-largest city, and soak in its vibrant atmosphere. Explore the harbor, climb Mt. Hlíðarfjall for panoramic views, and visit the Akureyri Art Museum for a dose of local talent. Savor fresh seafood at a family-run restaurant before settling into your cozy guesthouse.

Day 5: Dettifoss and the East Fjords

Wake up to the sound of crashing waves and take a scenic drive to Dettifoss, Europe's most powerful waterfall. Witness the raw power of this natural wonder before continuing to the East Fjords. Explore the charming village of Seyðisfjörður, renowned for its colorful houses and vibrant art scene. Visit Petra's Stone & Mineral Collection in Stöðvarfjörður, housing the world's largest zeolite collection, and lose yourself in the dramatic landscapes of Hengifoss and Fardagafoss waterfalls. Stay in a cozy cabin overlooking the fjord, enjoying the tranquility of this lesser-visited region.

Day 6: Landmannalaugar: Geothermal Oasis in the Highlands

Take a scenic route through the Laugavegur trail and prepare to be mesmerized by Landmannalaugar's otherworldly beauty. Hike through multicolored rhyolite mountains, swim in geothermal pools nestled amongst steaming vents, and soak in the breathtaking scenery. Choose a multi-day guided hike or experience the highlights on a day trip. Spend the night in a rustic mountain hut.

Day 7: South Coast Treasures and Reykjavik Return

Return to civilization, stopping at Vik to marvel at the black sand beach and Reynisdrangar sea stacks. Take a glacier hike on Sólheimajökull or explore the Skaftafell Ice Caves, venturing into the heart of a glacial world. Reach Reykjavik late afternoon and indulge in a celebratory farewell dinner, reminiscing about your off-the-beaten-path Icelandic adventure.

This Itinerary Is Just a Starting Point:

- Extend your stay in the Westfjords and hike the Hornstrandir Nature Reserve from start to finish.
- Experience the thrill of whitewater rafting on glacial rivers like Jökulsá or Þjórsá.
- Go stargazing in the remote highlands, where light pollution is minimal.
- Visit the remote island of Grímsey, the northernmost point of Iceland, and experience its unique island culture.

Remember:
- This itinerary requires renting a car for most parts.
- Off-the-beaten-path areas may have limited infrastructure and services. Be prepared with necessary camping or hiking gear.
- Booking accommodation in advance, especially in remote areas, is crucial.

Trading the familiar for the unexpected can lead to the most profound travel experiences. This off-the-beaten-path itinerary unlocks a different side of Iceland, waiting to be discovered by adventurous souls seeking raw beauty, solitude, and memories that will last a lifetime.

5-Day Reykjavik Rejuvenation: A Wellness Retreat in Iceland's Capital

Forget the rush of sightseeing and embrace a holistic approach to exploration with this five-day Reykjavik rejuvenation retreat. Immerse yourself in the city's vibrant yet relaxed atmosphere, focusing on mindfulness, self-care, and connecting with nature's restorative power.

Day 1: Arrive and Reconnect

After landing in Reykjavik, settle into your boutique hotel with spa access. Unwind with a geothermal soak or a soothing massage, releasing travel fatigue. Later, explore the charming streets of Laugavegur, browsing Icelandic design shops and savoring a healthy organic lunch at a local cafe.

Day 2: Geothermal Bliss and Nordic Rituals

Start your day with a yoga session overlooking the ocean, invigorating your body and mind. Next, visit the Secret Lagoon, a hidden geothermal pool nestled in a lava field. Relax in its milky blue waters, surrounded by steam and natural beauty. In the afternoon, join a "Sjavna Sigla" Nordic bath ritual, experiencing the contrast of a hot sauna followed by a plunge into the icy Atlantic. End the day with a delicious seafood dinner at a cozy harbor-side restaurant.

Day 3: Whale Watching and Coastal Tranquility

Embark on a morning whale-watching tour, sailing out into the North Atlantic in search of humpback whales, playful dolphins, and minke whales. Witness the majesty of these gentle giants in their natural habitat. Upon returning, wander along the scenic hiking trails of Grótta Lighthouse, enjoying the coastal breeze and panoramic views. Later, treat yourself to a spa treatment focused on Icelandic traditions, using volcanic minerals and seaweed extracts.

Day 4: Art, Culture, and Urban Nature

Immerse yourself in Reykjavik's cultural scene. Visit the National Gallery of Iceland for a dose of contemporary art, followed by a guided tour of the Reykjavik Art Museum. Explore the city's charming sculptures and street art, adding a touch of whimsy to your day. In the afternoon, escape the urban landscape and visit Laugavegur Botanical Garden, a haven of peaceful greenery showing Iceland's diverse flora. Enjoy a sunset picnic amid the vibrant flowers and tranquil ponds.

Day 5: Farewell and a Renewed You

Enjoy a final morning soak in your hotel's geothermal pool, reflecting on your exhilarating make-over experience. After a leisurely breakfast, wander through the bustling Kolaportið flea market, finding unusual souvenirs and soaking up the local atmosphere. Bid farewell to Reykjavik with a renewed sense of well-being, equipped with Icelandic self-care rituals and memories that will nourish your soul long after your journey ends.

Extras and Customization:

- Add a guided meditation session in a geothermal lagoon for complete relaxation.
- Visit Perlan, a rotating glass dome offering panoramic views and interactive exhibitions of natural wonders.
- Explore Reykjavik's vibrant coffee scene, discovering cozy cafes and unique brews.
- Take a day trip to the Blue Lagoon, indulging in its milky blue waters and luxurious spa treatments.

Remember:

- Plan your spa treatments and whale-watching tours to secure availability.
- Pack comfortable clothes for yoga, swimming, and exploring the city.
- Embrace the slower pace of Reykjavik and focus on mindfulness and self-care.
- Disconnect from technology and let the city's energy and natural beauty revitalize you.

This Reykjavik rejuvenation retreat offers a unique perspective on Iceland, focusing on your internal well-being while still experiencing the city's charm and natural wonders. Pack your yoga mat, your swimsuit, and an open mind, and prepare to return from Reykjavik feeling refreshed, reconnected, and ready to face the world with renewed energy.

Iceland awaits with open arms, ready to captivate your senses and forge memories that will last a lifetime. Whether you seek adrenaline-pumping adventures, cultural immersion, or simply a chance to reconnect with nature, Iceland has something for everyone. Choose your program, pack your bags, and prepare to be swept away by the magic of this land of fire and ice.

Bonus Chapter: Useful Icelandic Survival Phrases

Iceland, the land of fire and ice, beckons with its breathtaking landscapes, rich and ancient history, and intriguing culture. While English is widely spoken, learning a few key Icelandic phrases can enhance your experience and show respect to the locals. This bonus chapter provides a handy guide to essential phrases for navigating daily life in Iceland, from greetings and pleasantries to emergencies and specific travel needs.

Learning a few key Icelandic phrases can enhance your experience.
https://pixabay.com/photos/conversation-restaurant-pair-girls-1077974/

Basic Greetings and Politeness:
- **Hello:** Halló (HAH-loh).
- **Good Morning:** Góðan morgun (GO-than MOR-gun).
- **Good Afternoon/Evening:** Góðan daginn/kvöld (GO-than dah-gin/kvult).
- **Goodbye:** Bless (bles).
- **Thank You:** Takk (tahk).
- **You're Welcome:** Velkomin (vel-ko-min).
- **Please:** Vinsamlegast (VIN-sam-leh-gahst).
- **Excuse Me/Sorry:** Fyrirgefðu (FEER-ir-gev-thu).

Essential Phrases for Everyday Needs:
- **Do You Speak English?** Talar þú ensku? (tah-lar thoo en-skoo).
- **How Much Is This?** Hvað kostar þetta? (kvahð kos-tar thet-ta).
- **Where Is the Bathroom?** Hvar er baðherbergið? (kvar er bahth-her-ber-gið).
- **Can I Have The Bill, Please?** Má ég fá reikninginn, takk? (mah ayg FAH rey-king-in, tahk).
- **I Would Like...:** Ég vildi... (ayg vil-di).
- **One, Two, Three:** Einn, tveir, þrír (ayn, tveyr, thrir).

Travel and Transportation:
- **Where Is the Bus Stop/Train Station?** Hvar er stöðin / lestarsstöðin? (kvar er stoh-din/les-tar-stoh-din).
- **Can I Get a Ticket to...?** Get ég miða til...? (get ayg mi-tha til...).
- **Can I Rent a Car?** Get ég leigt bíl? (get ayg leygt bil).
- **Where Is the Parking Lot?** Hvar er bílastæðið? (kvar er bi-la-steh-thith).
- **I Need Help with My Luggage:** Ég þarf hjálp með farangurinn mínum. (ayg tharf hyalp meth FAH-rang-ur-in mi-num).

Dining and Food:
- **Can I Have a Table for...?:** Get ég borð fyrir...? (get ayg borð fir...).
- **The Menu, Please:** Sjáðu matseðli, takk. (syau mat-se-tli, tahk).
- **What Do You Recommend?** Hvað mælir þú til? (kvahð MAY-lir thoo til).

- **I'm Allergic to...**: Ég er ofsaklæddur við... (ayg er oh-fuh-klaet-thur við...).
- **The Check, Please**: Reikninginn, takk. (rey-king-in, tahk).

Emergencies and Help:
- **Help!**: Hjálp! (HYALP).
- **Can You Help Me?**: Getur þú hjálpað mér? (GEH-tur thoo HYAL-pa-th meer?).
- **I Need a Doctor/Police**: Ég þarf lækni/lögguna. (ayg tharf lehk-ni/lohg-gu-na).
- **Where Is the Nearest Hospital?**: Hvar er næsta sjúkrahús? (kvar er nay-sta sju-kra-hus).
- **I Lost My Passport**: Ég hætti vegabréfinu mínu. (ayg hæt-ti ve-ga-bre-fi-nu mi-nu).

Bonus Phrases:
- **Cheers!**: Skál! (skol).
- **Beautiful!**: Fallegt! (fah-legt).
- **Thank You for Your Hospitality**: Takk fyrir gestagjafinn. (tahk fir gehs-ta-giaf-fin).
- **I Hope to See You Again**: Ég vona að sjá þig aftur. (ayg vo-na aht syau thig aftur).

Pronunciation Tips:

Icelandic pronunciation might seem daunting at first, but with a few key tips, you can master the basics.

- **Double Consonants:** Pronounce them with a stronger emphasis than in English. For example, "Takk" (thank you) is pronounced "tahk" with a hard "k" sound.
- **Vowels:** "a" is similar to "ah" in "father," "e" like "eh" in "bed," "i" like "ee" in "see," "o" like "oh" in "so," and "u" like "oo" in "moon."
- **R:** Pronounced like a guttural "h" at the back of the throat.
- **Th:** Pronounced like "th" in "think."
- **ð:** Similar to the "th" in "the," but voiced.
- **Stress:** Usually falls on the first syllable of a word.

Additional Resources:
- **Online Pronunciation Guides:** There are many online resources available that offer audio recordings of Icelandic phrases, making it easier to hear and practice the correct pronunciation.
- **Icelandic Language Apps:** Several apps are available that can help you learn basic Icelandic vocabulary and phrases.
- **Phrasebooks:** While not essential with the current prevalence of English, a pocket-sized Icelandic phrasebook can be a helpful tool for travelers.
- **Duolingo:** This user-friendly app offers an interactive Icelandic course with audio pronunciation guides.
- **Forvo:** This online dictionary allows you to hear native speakers say various Icelandic words and phrases.
- **Icelandic Phrasebook:** Invest in a pocket-sized phrasebook for quick reference and confidence during your trip.

By putting in a little effort and taking advantage of these resources, you can open up a deeper understanding and appreciation of Icelandic culture and make your Icelandic adventure even more enriching. Don't be afraid to make mistakes. Icelanders appreciate the effort of visitors trying to speak their language. Start with a few basic phrases and gradually expand your vocabulary. Have fun and enjoy the process of learning Icelandic.

Appendix: Unveiling Treasures from A to Z

Iceland beckons with a kaleidoscope of wonders – from steaming geothermal pools to soaring glaciers and moss-carpeted lava fields to vibrant cultural havens. To navigate this tapestry of treasures, embark on an Icelandic odyssey guided by this A-to-Z itinerary, tailor-made for your thirst for adventure and cultural immersion.

A:
- **Akureyri Art Museum:** Dive into the vibrant art scene of Iceland's second city, where contemporary Icelandic and international works ignite your imagination.
- **Akureyri Botanical Garden:** Wander through Iceland's largest botanical garden, a tranquil oasis planted with native flora and exotic plants from around the world.
- **Alþingishúsið (Parliament House):** Witness the heart of Icelandic democracy at this historic building in Reykjavik, standing tall as a symbol of the nation's independence.

B:
- **Blue Lagoon:** Immerse yourself in the milky blue serenity of this geothermal oasis, surrounded by volcanic rock and pampered by nature's warm embrace.
- **Borgarfjörður Eystri region:** Explore the dramatic landscapes of this east coast region, home to the iconic Kirkjufell mountain and

the picturesque waterfall Kvernáfoss.

- **Brunnstadsvegurinn Sculpture Route:** Embark on a scenic drive along this sculpture route in South Iceland, where contemporary art blends seamlessly with the wild landscapes.

C:

- **Dettifoss Waterfall:** Witness the raw power of Europe's most powerful waterfall, a thunderous cascade plunging into a rugged canyon, leaving you breathless.
- **Diamond Beach:** Marvel at the glistening icebergs scattered across the black sand beach near Jökulsárlón glacier lagoon, each a shimmering gem sculpted by nature.
- **Churchill National Park:** Hike through breathtaking valleys and encounter diverse wildlife in this north-central park, a haven for arctic foxes, reindeer, and ptarmigans.

D:

- **Gullfoss Waterfall:** The Golden Falls shimmer under the Icelandic sun, a majestic double cascade framed by rainbows and ancient myths.
- **Grjótagjá Geothermal Cave:** Step back in time into this natural cave with a geothermal pool inside, where early Icelanders once bathed in the warm waters.
- **Glacier Lagoon Boat Tours:** Sail amongst glistening icebergs in Jökulsárlón or Vatnajökull glacier lagoon, experiencing the mesmerizing beauty of glacial ice up close.

H:

- **Hallgrímskirkja Church:** Ascend the iconic tower of Reykjavik's landmark church, soaking in panoramic views of the city and the vast Icelandic landscape.
- **Hornstrandir Nature Reserve:** Discover the remote wilderness of this Westfjords peninsula, hiking through dramatic cliffs and meadows teeming with wildflowers and maybe catching a glimpse of the elusive Arctic foxes.
- **Hvitserkur Rock Formation:** Stand in awe before this towering white rock formation near Akureyri, resembling a troll frozen in time, guarding the coastline.

I:
- **Ísafjörður Town:** Nestled in the Westfjords, this charming port town exudes a timeless charm, its colorful houses reflecting on the fjord – like a live watercolor painting.
- **Íslenskar þjóðsagnasafn (National Folklore Museum):** Immerse yourself in Icelandic folklore and mythology at this museum in Reykjavik, filled with captivating stories of elves, trolls, and hidden worlds.
- **Ice Cave Tours:** Venture into the icy heart of the Vatnajökull glacier, exploring mesmerizing blue caves sculpted by nature's forces, a truly unforgettable experience.

J:
- **Jökulsárlón Glacier Lagoon:** Sail among glistening icebergs in this otherworldly lagoon, their crystalline forms sculpted by nature's glacial artistry.
- **Jokulsarlon Ice Caves:** Enter awe-inspiring caves carved within the Vatnajökull glacier, their translucent ceilings shimmering under the glacial ice, an ethereal world of light and ice.
- **Jokulsarlon Glacier Hike:** Embark on an unforgettable adventure, trekking across the vast Vatnajökull glacier and witnessing its awe-inspiring crevasses, icefalls, and glacial lakes.

K:
- **Landmannalaugar Geothermal Area:** Hike through a rainbow-hued wonderland of rhyolite mountains, volcanic craters, and steaming vents, a feast for the senses.
- **Kverkfjöll Mountains:** Challenge yourself with a mountaineering adventure in this rugged eastern mountain range, conquering its sharp peaks and witnessing breathtaking panoramas.
- **Kerlingarfjöll Geothermal Area:** Hike through a surreal landscape of colorful rhyolite mountains, bubbling mud pools, and steaming fumaroles in this central highland region.

L:
- **Lake Myvatn:** Explore the otherworldly beauty of this volcanic landscape, dotted with geothermal vents, bubbling mud pools, and diverse bird life.

- **Grænavatn Turf Farm:** Step back in time at this traditional turf farm near Mývatn, experiencing a slice of Icelandic history and traditional farming practices.
- **Laugavegur Hiking Trail:** Embark on a multi-day trek through the majestic landscape of Landman.

M:

- **Mývatn Nature Baths:** Float in geothermal bliss amid the stark beauty of Lake Myvatn, indulging in a restorative soak surrounded by lava fields.
- **Maritime Museum (Reykjavik):** Learn about Iceland's rich maritime history at this museum, with exhibits showcasing traditional fishing boats, historical artifacts, and stories of daring seafarers.
- **Museum of Design and Applied Art (Reykjavík):** Immerse yourself in Icelandic design and craftsmanship at this museum, from intricate textiles and furniture to contemporary works that blend tradition with innovation.

N:

- **Natural History Museum (Vatnið í náttúru Íslands)(Reykjavík):** Dive into Iceland's fascinating natural history, from its volcanic origins to its unique flora and fauna, at this interactive museum.
- **North Iceland Folk Museum (Akureyri):** Learn about the traditions and everyday life of Icelanders in the north at this museum, with exhibits of historical tools, clothing, and household items.
- **Northern Lights Tours:** Witness the breathtaking aurora borealis dance across the night sky on a guided tour, a mesmerizing spectacle best enjoyed in remote areas far from light pollution.

O:

- **Öræfi Mountains:** Trek through the crown jewels of Iceland's highlands, where glaciers glisten on top of jagged peaks and the wind whispers ancient tales.
- **Seljavellir Geothermal Field:** Hike through a geothermal wonderland near Thingvellir National Park, witnessing bubbling mud pools, colorful hot springs, and steam-blowing fumaroles.

P:

- **Outdoor Museums:** Discover Iceland's unique history and cultural heritage through open-air museums like Glaumbaer Skútustaðir turf farm in Skagafjörður or Arbaer Open Air Museum in Reykjavik.
- **Petra's Stone & Mineral Collection:** Marvel at the world's largest zeolite collection, housed in a former farmhouse, each gem a testament to Iceland's volcanic heart.
- **Puffin Tours:** Go on a boat tour and watch adorable puffins nesting along the cliffs of Vestmannaeyjar or other coastal areas, capturing their playful antics and striking colors.
- **Skaftafell National Park:** Explore the diverse landscapes of this southern park, from glaciers and ice caves to black sand beaches and cascading waterfalls.

R:

- **Reynisdrangar Sea Stacks:** Stand awestruck before these basalt giants rising from the Atlantic Ocean, their dramatic silhouettes outlined against the vibrant colors of the sky.
- **Reykjavík City Hall:** Discover the architectural gem of Reykjavík City Hall, with its striking design and panoramic views from the observation deck.
- **Reykjanes Peninsula:** Explore the geothermal wonders of this peninsula near Reykjavik, from Gunnuhver hot springs to Reykjanesbaer GeoPark and the Blue Lagoon.

S:

- **Seljalandsfoss Waterfall:** Feel the spray on your face as you stand behind the cascading curtain of Seljalandsfoss, as its power and beauty become etched in your memory.
- **Skógafoss Waterfall:** Witness the thunderous Skógafoss waterfall cascading into the ocean, a powerful spectacle framed by rainbows and ancient myths.
- **Secret Lagoon:** Immerse yourself in the lesser-known geothermal pool of the Secret Lagoon, nestled in the lava fields, which offers a more intimate experience than the Blue Lagoon.

T:

- **Þingvellir National Park:** Explore this UNESCO World Heritage Site where tectonic plates diverge. Dive between continents in crystal-clear waters and stand on the ancient grounds of Iceland's first parliament.
- **Thorvaldseyri Volcano:** Hike to the summit of this active volcano in South Iceland, witnessing the crater's colorful geothermal activity and panoramic views.
- **Thermal Pools (Various Locations):** Soak in the warm embrace of Iceland's numerous geothermal pools, from Laugarvatn Fontana in South Iceland to the Secret Lagoon near Reykjavik.

U:

- **Vatnajökull National Park:** Hike through Europe's largest national park, the realm of glaciers, ice caves, volcanic craters, and endless horizons.
- **Underwater Snorkeling and Diving:** Explore the hidden world beneath the surface in the Silfra Fissure in Thingvellir National Park or other geothermal pools, bumping into unusual aquatic life and seeing a wondrous underwater landscape.
- **Urban Art Tours:** Discover Reykjavik's vibrant street art scene with guided tours showcasing murals, sculptures, and installations that reflect the city's creative spirit.

V:

- **Vik Village:** Explore the southernmost village in Iceland; its black sand beach and Reynisdrangar sea stacks paint a dramatic coastal scene.
- **Vestmannaeyjar Islands:** Take a ferry or boat tour to these volcanic islands off the South Coast, where you'll see puffins, caves, and the remnants of a volcanic eruption.
- **Volcano Museum (Skógar):** Learn about Iceland's volcanic history and eruptions at this museum situated near Skógafoss waterfall, with rocks, artifacts, and amazing interactive exhibits.
- **Viking World (Reykjavík):** Immerse yourself in the Viking Age at this interactive museum, reliving their daily lives, exploring replica ships, and witnessing demonstrations of crafts and combat.

- **Vatnajökull Glacier Jeep Tour:** Go on an off-road adventure on the vast Vatnajökull glacier, traversing ice fields and crevasses and discovering hidden ice caves, a thrilling experience for the adventurous.

W:

- **Westfjords:** Venture off the beaten path and explore the rugged beauty of the Westfjords, with its hidden coves, charming fishing villages, dramatic fjords, and diverse wildlife.
- **Whale Watching Tours:** Sail the Icelandic waters and cross paths with majestic whales and dolphins in their natural habitat, from humpbacks and minke whales to playful porpoises and orcas.
- **Whales of Iceland Museum (Husavik):** Learn about Iceland's diverse whale species and their conservation at this museum in Husavik, a town known as the whale-watching capital of Europe.

Y:

- **Ytri-Búðardalur village:** Step back in time in this remote Westfjords village, where traditional turf houses and a slow pace of life offer a glimpse into Iceland's past.

Z:

- **Zoo of South Iceland (Reykjavík):** Visit native Icelandic animals like Arctic foxes, puffins, and reindeer at this family-friendly zoo, learning about their unique adaptations and conservation efforts.
- **Zodiac Boat Tours:** Sail among the icebergs of Jökulsárlón or Vatnajökull glacier lagoon on a zodiac boat, getting closer to the ice formations and experiencing the glacial landscape from a unique perspective.

This A to Z list provides a comprehensive guide to Icelandic attractions, monuments, and museums, offering something for every interest and travel style. Remember, this is just a starting point. Tailor your itinerary to your passions and timeframe, and be prepared to be captivated by the magic of Iceland at every turn. Happy travels!

If you enjoyed this book, a review on Amazon would be greatly appreciated because it would mean a lot to hear from you.

To leave a review:
1. Open your camera app.
2. Point your mobile device at the QR code.
3. The review page will appear in your web browser.

Thanks for your support!

Welcome Aboard, Discover Your Limited-Time Free Bonus!

Hello, traveler! Welcome to the Captivating Travels family, and thanks for grabbing a copy of this book! Since you've chosen to join us on this journey, we'd like to offer you something special.

Check out the link below for a FREE Ultimate Travel Checklist eBook & Printable PDF to make your travel planning stress-free and enjoyable.

But that's not all - you'll also gain access to our exclusive email list with even more free e-books and insider travel tips. Well, what are you waiting for? Click the link below to join and embark on your next adventure with ease.

Access your bonus here:
https://livetolearn.lpages.co/checklist/
Or, Scan the QR code!

Check out another book in the series

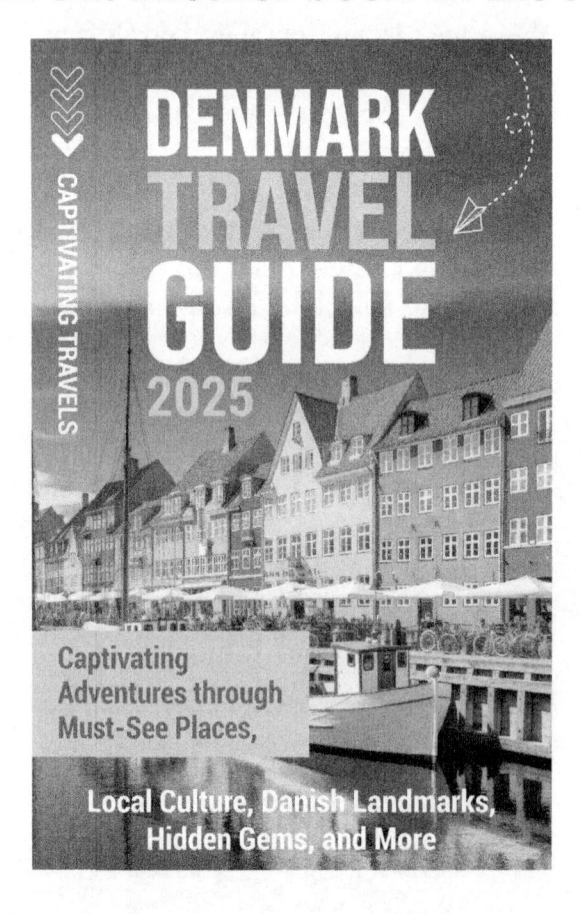

References

Catherine. (2023, June 4). The Best Off-the-Beaten-Path Things to Do in Iceland. Nordic Visitor. https://www.nordicvisitor.com/blog/iceland-hidden-gems-off-the-beaten-path/

Charlotte. (2022, January 3). 13 Hidden Gems in Iceland (MAP Included). Charlie's Wanderings. https://charlieswanderings.com/destinations/europe/hidden-gems-in-iceland/

Gillies, E. (2021, December 21). These are the 10 best places to visit in North Iceland. Nordic Visitor. https://www.nordicvisitor.com/blog/in-focus-8-must-sees-in-north-iceland/

Gunnarsdóttir, N. (n.d.). 20 Hidden Gems in Iceland: Go Off-the-Beaten-Path. Guide to Iceland. https://guidetoiceland.is/best-of-iceland/20-hidden-gems-in-iceland

Hamper, A. (2019). 18 Top-Rated Tourist Attractions in Iceland | PlanetWare. Planetware. https://www.planetware.com/tourist-attractions/iceland-isl.htm

Iceland. (2022, March 23). Iceland Geography Facts and Country Profile: Mountain Peaks, Ice Fields, and Plateaus. Iceland. https://www.iceland.org/geography/

Iceland Like a Local. (n.d.). Discover Iceland Destinations Sorted by Great Regions. Iceland like a Local. https://www.iceland-like-a-local.com/regions

Iceland on the Web. (n.d.). Iceland Regions – Iceland On The Web. Iceland on the Web. https://www.icelandontheweb.com/articles-on-iceland/iceland-regions

Igor. (2023, June 15). 25 Hidden Gems in Iceland Nobody Writes About. Epic Iceland. https://epiciceland.net/hidden-gems-iceland/

Thrillophilia. (2016, March 11). 40 Places to Visit in Iceland, Tourist Places & Top Attractions. Thrillophilia.

https://www.thrillophilia.com/destinations/iceland/places-to-visit

Visit Iceland. (n.d.-a). Geography of Iceland – the Land of Ice and Fire. Visit Iceland. https://www.visiticeland.com/article/geography-of-iceland_1/

Visit Iceland. (n.d.-b). The Regions – North Iceland. Visit Iceland. https://www.visiticeland.com/the-regions/the-north/

Printed in Great Britain
by Amazon